Foreword

CW00338210

Islands represent freedom, independence and creativity. They appear and disappear over time, according to weather events, water flow and intervention by people. Islands have an enduring and often romantic appeal. Being closer to nature, at the mercy of the elements and somewhere as distinctive as an island makes us feel alive.

Often associated with seas and oceans, fewer people realise there are islands on rivers too. When we discovered there are up to 200 islands on the River Thames – the iconic river that runs through the centre of London and beyond – we had to find out more.

A surprising number of the islands on the River Thames are inhabited. Often home to creative communities and those who enjoy living unconventional lifestyles, London's islanders are intrepid and spirited, with remarkable vision. They've set up home and live full, inspiring and original lives in the middle of the river. While some can drive or walk to their homes via bridges, others row in boats, reaching the mainland under their own steam.

Home to musicians, artists, entrepreneurs, film industry experts, sports stars and business people – not to mention plenty of normal families – the communities on London's islands share something greater than their professions. They have an affinity with the water and seek a feeling of space from the rest of the world. They're 'yes' people who don't worry about convention.

Each and every River Thames island has a story to tell. Music is a recurrent theme on the islands – a place where creativity can reign supreme away from the restrictions of the mainland. Legends ranging from David ___ The Rolling Stones and The Beatles, to Eric Clapton, Pink Floyd and Black Sabbath, have all hung out on London's islands. Charlie Chaplin was first discovered on a grand houseboat moored to a River Thames island. There are stories about royals and politicians hiding out on the islands, and one such island supposedly had a tunnel for a well-known public figure to reach the local pub from his island hideout! London's islands have also been the locations of events that have forever changed the course of history, as unparalleled locations where delicate matters can be discussed without fear of intrusion.

This is a book of lives lived in the extraordinary setting of the River Thames islands. They may not have palm trees or white sandy beaches, but each one of London's islands has an idyllic appeal in its own way. We follow the river from Canvey Island in Essex to Monkey Island in Berkshire, uncovering incredible stories of extraordinary events from centuries past, and hearing from the people who live on the islands today.

We want you to feel inspired by those who actively choose the unexpected. Whether you find a city island to live on like our friends in this book, or take some of their spirit away with you, choosing a different way of living can be positively liberating. Island dreams are possible – even in the city.

Sascha Mengerink, Publisher
Sasha Arms, Editor

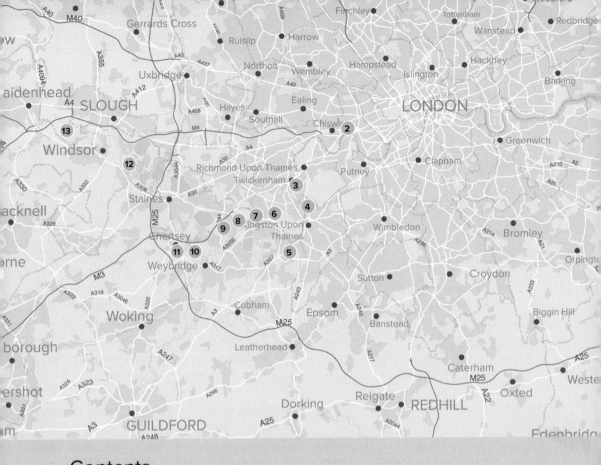

Contents

MAGNA CARTA ISLAND

Canvey Island

This huge island has a kitsch and quirky seaside feeling to it, given its location right by the North Sea. Numerous salt marshes and retro-cool amusement parks such as Fantasy Island add to the island's charm. The entire island used to be marshland, although it has a long human history too. Everything from Viking longboats to Roman pottery have been discovered over the years. There's a proud Dutch heritage on the island too, after a group of Dutch builders were invited to live on the island and build sea defences and drainage ditches in the 17th century. Today, the island's museum can be found in the old Dutch Cottage.

There was no bridge onto the island until 1931, so the large island previously had a small population and a faraway feeling. Historians described it as the 'world's end', while its remoteness gained it a reputation as a hideout for river smugglers in the 1800s.

In the 1900s, Canvey Island became a tourist destination, as the only one of the River Thames islands to offer wide sandy beaches and a true seaside feeling. Campsites and holiday chalets sprang up alongside lots of amenities. Ove Arup – the designer of the Sydney Opera House – even designed a waterside eatery, The Labworth. It's still there today and is now a Grade II listed building.

Believe it or not, Canvey Island even has its own monster. In the 1950s, the carcasses of two unidentifiable sea creatures washed up on the island. One was more than a metre in length and while there has been speculation about the species, it was never formally identified...

Nowadays, Canvey Island has a combination of large industries, residences and holiday chalets, although on a much lesser scale than during the island's golden era. The famous sea walls have an eclectic combination of murals that various artists were commissioned to design. In recent years, the island has been found to have one of the highest levels of biodiversity in western Europe. The 16th century Lobster Smack inn – featured in *Great Expectations* by Charles Dickens – is still standing, while the island enjoys a more recent music history. Lee Brilleaux, the frontman of Dr Feelgood, grew up on the island and formed the band there in the 1970s. For 20 years after his death in 1994, fans flocked to Canvey Island to do a memorial walk in his honour.

Size and location:
Approximate size: 18,540,000m²
Coordinates: 51.517, 0.578
Can you visit? Yes, just drive over the bridge.

Carl's tips:
Enjoy the art and bracing winds by the sea walls, grab a bite in The Labworth (Furtherwick Road, SS8 7DW) and then get lost on a walk in West Canvey Marsh: a wetland reserve and the largest single area of green space on the island.

Dean Macey

Athlete

*A former Olympics and Commonwealth Games decathlete hailing from Canvey Island,
'The Dean Machine' is now a television presenter and athletics consultant.*

How did your family end up on Canvey Island?

My family is originally from the East End of London and Canvey Island was a popular holiday spot for people from that neck of the woods. My parents used to holiday on the island and they loved it so much, they decided to move here in 1976. I was born in 1977, so Canvey Island always been home to me.

Tell us how your early life on the island led to you becoming an international sports champion.

I wasn't academic as a kid; all I wanted to do was play sport. I used to get thrown out of the classroom all the time for getting into mischief. I was sent over to the sports teacher, Mr Taylor, who couldn't control me either, so he would send me onto the astroturf to practice my triple jump. All those years of being thrown out of the classroom led to me winning a national triple jumping title! Mr Taylor's one of my best friends now too.

You went on to win the Commonwealth Games decathlon, you've won two World Championship medals and you finished fourth in the Olympic Games twice. What was returning to Canvey Island like after those events?

Coming home made all of my achievements much more special. I'd done all these major championships and I'd been everywhere from the Olympic Village to the Commonwealth Games Village. It was obvious I'd achieved something quite special but when I was in those places, I didn't really know anyone who came up to me to say 'congratulations'. When I came back to Canvey Island and walked down the High Street, people I knew came up to me, telling me how I'd inspired their kids. I did it because I wanted to see how good I could be, but when I came home, I realised how much of a difference I'd made to other people. It was amazing!

How did the Canvey Island community welcome you home as a champion?

The island gave me a great sense of camaraderie. When I came back from a major championship and I'd done well, there were banners everywhere around the island saying 'Congratulations Deano!' A pub called The Silver Jubilee – which has now closed down – changed its name to The Silver Decathlete for a month! They gave me 100 free pints to celebrate my success and they were drunk in one night by me and some friends. Another time I was driving along the road when a bus stopped in front of me. Every single person on the bus poured out and surrounded my car! The island's got a close-knit community spirit that gave me a real sense of achievement.

What are you working on nowadays?

I spend half of my time working on fishing television programmes, presenting shows such as *The Big Fish Off* and *Fishing Allstars* for ITV. I've also had programmes on the Discovery Channel and Sky Sports. Throughout the summer, I do athletics consultancy, trying to improve knowledge and techniques in grassroots athletics. When I was a kid, I was fed a lot of bad information and wrong techniques. I'm very passionate about trying to instil the good stuff early on. I'm not saying it's going to transform anyone's life, but it certainly makes things easier for those who follow similar career paths to become professional athletes.

You travel frequently for your work. What makes Canvey Island feel like home when you return?

I've travelled all over the UK and the world, but I've never felt like anywhere else could be home. I wouldn't say it's spectacular. When I tell people I live on an island, I always have a joke about it having its own microclimate and palm trees on the beach. That's definitely not true! My favourite part of the island is the athletics track. Of all the places I've been to in the world and of all the things I've done, there's nowhere else I'd rather be when I'm on that track. I don't think a number actually exists for the times I've run around it! But it never gets old or boring.

Describe Canvey Island.

During the week it's like a little London, but at the weekend it's got a very chilled and relaxed holiday feeling about it. On the weekends when the sun is shining, it's absolutely magic. You could genuinely live your entire life and never leave the island. If you don't like driving, change or travel, the island has everything you need, even though it's only two miles wide and five miles long! My wife's parents were born and bred on Canvey Island as well and I've seen photos of them as kids when the island just had fields. It's so built up now it's hard to imagine, but there are still quiet bits of the island to discover.

What are your favourite Canvey Island childhood memories?

Cherry Stores was a tiny sweet shop next to The Oysterfleet, where Dr Feelgood used to play. Everybody used to meet there after school to get their sweets. It's not there anymore, but every time I drive past, it's still there in my heart! Sometimes after school, we'd grab some fishing gear from my mate's garage and go fishing on Canvey Lake. Those were the days when your parents didn't worry if you turned up a couple of hours late after leaving school.

What's the worst thing about living on Canvey Island nowadays?

Traffic! When I was a kid, my parents used to moan about rush hour, which was literally just an hour. Now it seems to go on for three hours! With my job, I'm blessed that I leave before the traffic kicks in and I come home after it's calmed down again.

Where should visitors to Canvey Island head to?

The seafront is pretty cool. The sea walls have a memorial section where there are loads of professional artworks. I like the wall for a family-run charity I'm the patron of, The Indee Rose Trust.

Where do you see yourself in the future?

Whenever I drive onto Canvey Island, I know I'm home. So I'll probably still be here in 50 years' time, if we haven't sunk!

Find out more about Dean on Twitter @DeanMacey

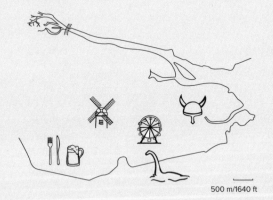

500 m/1640 ft

CANVEY ISLAND

Thorney Island

Right in the political heart of London, Westminster used to be on an island called Thorney Island. This is where Westminster Abbey and the Palace of Westminster – now known as the Houses of Parliament – were built. It was originally an inhospitable place full of thorny vegetation, hence the name 'Thorney Island', which monks gradually tamed over the years. The level of the land rose, small streams were built over and the Thames was embanked. Eventually, Thorney Island was no longer visible. The only remnants of the name can be seen in Thorney Street, behind the MI5 building, and in The Thorney Island Society, a local heritage organisation.

Size and location:
Approximate size: 121,406m²
Coordinates: 51.499, -0.126

Can you visit?
Yes, no boat needed nowadays!

Carl's tips:
Get an idea of the scale of the former Thorney Island by visiting two points thought to mark its boundaries. Grosvenor Canal – which doesn't actually go anywhere nowadays – marks one edge of the island, while the lake in St James's Park marks the other edge. It should take around half an hour to walk between the two. Thames River Boats (www.wpsa.co.uk) have various boat routes with destinations between Westminster and Hampton Court, where you can take in some of the islands on this stretch of the river.

200 m/656 ft

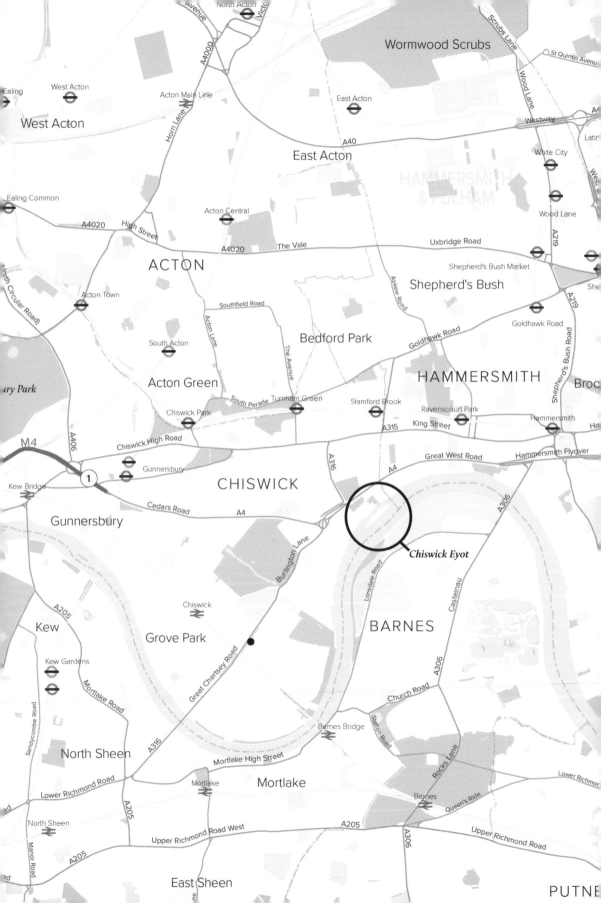

Chiswick Eyot

Curious visitors can walk from the riverbank to this uninhabited island at low tide. At high tide, it's completely submerged. The island was used during the industrial revolution for growing grass and osier willows for basket making. Nowadays, Chiswick Eyot is a local nature reserve. The island made the news in 2010 when a pensioner claimed to be living on the island, sleeping in a net in the trees to avoid the incoming tide. Volunteer groups help to maintain the vegetation on the island and some talented basket makers still use the willows to make their creations. During the summer, the shingle beach is an idyllic place to sit with a cold drink. Beware – the tide can rise quickly – so educate yourself about the tides before wandering over.

Size and location:
Approximate size: 9,000m²
Coordinates: 51.487, -0.245

Can you visit?
Walk there at low tide at your own risk.

Carl's tips:
If you prefer to stay on solid ground, get a view of Chiswick Eyot from the junction of Chiswick Mall and Chiswick Lane South. Just a 10 minute walk downriver is The Old Ship W6 (25 Upper Mall, W6 9TD), a gorgeous 18th century riverside pub. You can also walk along the Thames Path on the other side of the river to get a glimpse of the island. Continue along the path to get lost in the Leg O Mutton nature reserve.

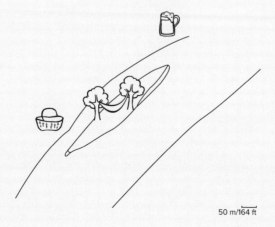

50 m/164 ft

Lois Walpole
Artist

*This artist and basket maker is a graduate of Central Saint Martins School of Art, the
London College of Furniture and the Royal College of Art. She discovered Chiswick Eyot when
collecting materials for her basket making.*

Introduce yourself.

I am an artist and basket maker. The techniques and forms of basket making are the inspiration for my work, which manifests itself as both installations and functional objects.

How did you discover Chiswick Eyot?

I first learned about the eyot from Tony Kirkham in 2002. At the time, he was responsible for the arboretum and horticultural services at the Royal Botanic Gardens, Kew and he had just agreed to let me plant my living willow experiments in the nursery there. I was doing my PhD at the Royal College of Art at the time, trying to prove that it was possible to grow furniture. I needed to get hold of some living willow cuttings for the experiments. Tony told me about a little island on the Thames covered in pollarded willows, which he thought basket makers used to cut. It sounded incredible to me. I had lived in London for 28 years – using willow for much of that time – yet I knew nothing about it.

Describe the feeling on the island.

The eyot is a very special place because you can only get to it at low tide. Pollarded willows cover the island, creating a mini forest in summertime. The stunted skeletons of the two metre high boles in winter are a strange sight in London too. Underfoot is a deep carpet of twiggy material, matted with thousands of tiny pieces of plastic waste that floats in when the eyot is covered by high tides. This flotsam eventually meshes with the leaves and twigs – shed from the willows – and together they form the surface of the island. The tide at the eyot rips in and out quickly, so any visits are tinged with a sense of adventure because of the very real prospect of finding yourself alone on an island in the middle of the Thames. You have to stay alert.

What did you make with the osiers you collected on Chiswick Eyot?

The osiers I gathered were planted at Kew and eventually became a living table, chairs and other functional things. It was displayed as an exhibition called Grown Home in 2003. My most successful home grown willow object was a coat hanger. It was planted, grafted and eventually cut off the plant and used in my wardrobe.

What advice would you give to people hoping to discover some of the islands on the River Thames?

Make sure you have a good map and tide table and know how to read both. Ensure you have something to tell the time by. Also wear sturdy boots because unfortunately there can be sharp and dangerous objects in amongst the flotsam. Finally, check that the island you are visiting is not private property.

Describe your lasting impression of Chiswick Eyot.

For me, knowing this was a place where willow was grown specifically for basket makers was just magic. Although we know from maps that small willow holts could be found all over London, I know of no others that remain. History was living and breathing for me the day I first visited the eyot and I will never forget the sense of being in such close contact with the past.

Find out more about Lois Walpole at www.loiswalpole.com

Oliver's Island

Legend has it that this uninhabited island was named after Oliver Cromwell, a controversial military and political leader in the 1600s. The story goes that Cromwell once took refuge on the island and that he built a tunnel from The Bulls Head pub on the mainland to the island. It's likely this is just an old myth, but it can't be ruled out entirely... A smithy was built on the island in the 1800s and a barge was moored alongside it, from which tolls were collected from passing boats. The City Barge pub on the riverbank took its name from this piece of barging history. The Port of London Authority tried to sell the island in 1971, but the local Strand-on-the-Green Association protested; the plans were subsequently dropped. The island is nowadays thickly wooded, attracting herons, other birds, and maybe, just maybe, the odd politician who needs a bit of peace and quiet....

Size and location:
Approximate size: 2,000m²
Coordinates: 51.485, -0.281

Can you visit?
Yes, but it's only accessible by boat.

Carl's tips:
There are occasional guided tours of Oliver's Island during Thames Tidefest (www. thamestidefest.net) every September. From the riverbank, get a great view of Oliver's Island from Strand-On-The Green...and then have a drink in The Bull's Head (15 Strand-On-The-Green, W4 3PQ) or the City Barge (27 Strand-On-The-Green, W4 3PH). And if you're curious about Oliver Cromwell's tunnel, we're sure the proprietors of The Bull's Head are used to people closely inspecting the floor... For a quieter glimpse of the island, walk along the Thames Path on the other side of the river.

20 m/66 ft

Brentford Ait

This uninhabited island sometimes appears to be two islands, as a lower piece of ground in the middle of the island is covered by water at high tide. In the 18th century there was a pub on the island called the Three Swans, which seems to have existed in some form for close to 100 years, although any trace of it is long gone today. Around this time too, the island is said to have been a meeting place for the future King George IV and the actress Mary ('Perdita') Robinson. In the late 19th century, there was a tree planting drive on the island, so that visitors of Kew Gardens on one side could not see the industrialised area of Brentford on the other side. The island is still full of large trees today. Brentford Ait is only accessible by boat – don't be tempted to cross on foot at low tide, as the mud is quick sinking.

Size and location:
Approximate size: 26,419m²
Coordinates: 51.486, -0.293

Can you visit?
Yes, but it's only accessible by boat.

Carl's tips:
Get the best view of the island from the Kew side of the river, on the section of the Thames Path that runs parallel to Ferry Lane. While you're in the area, make the most of what Kew has to offer, including Kew Gardens, a selection of good-looking pubs and cricket on the green during the summer.

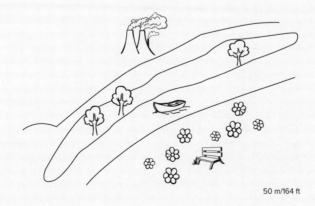

50 m/164 ft

Lot's Ait

Next door to Brentford Ait, Lot's Ait is accessible by a footbridge. The island is home to a former yard where barges were repaired. After a period of closure, John's Boat Works (www.lotsait.com) commenced boat building again in 2012. There have been various plans to develop the island over the years – including to build a restaurant and leisure facilities – none of which have come into fruition. Believe it or not, Lot's Ait was used to film African river scenes for the 1951 film, *The African Queen*. Starring Humphrey Bogart and Katharine Hepburn, this is the only film Bogart won an Oscar for. More recently, some scenes from the Dominic Cooper film about a Special Boat Service commando – *Stratton* – were filmed there.

Size and location:
Approximate size: 4,738m²
Coordinates: 51.485, -0.298

Can you visit?
Yes, just walk across the footbridge.

Carl's tips:
On the riverbank near the Lot's Ait footbridge is Watermans Arts Centre, with a vibrant cultural calendar and film showings in its independent cinema.

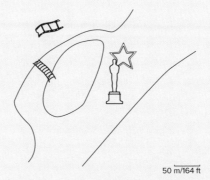

50 m/164 ft

The '

Id Road

The Avenue

h Parade Turnha

ISWICK

Burlington

High Street

Mortlak

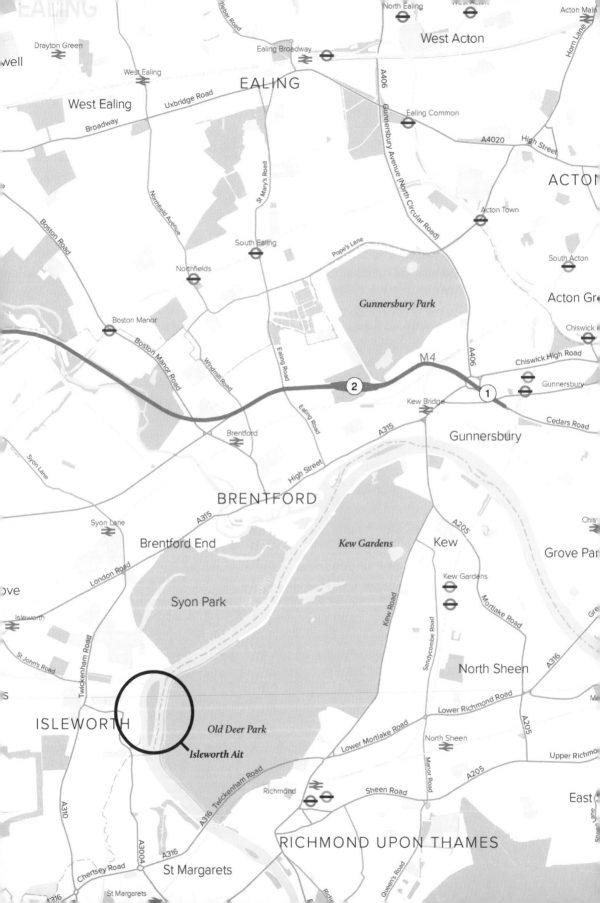

Isleworth Ait

An officially designated Local Nature Reserve because of the huge diversity of wildlife on this island, Isleworth Ait is rarely visited, except by a team of volunteers from the London Wildlife Trust. The island was previously part of the Syon Park Estate, owned by the Duke of Northumberland. Long before that, there is some evidence to show the Vikings may have camped on the island too. In the last couple of centuries, the island was sometimes referred to as 'London's basket', as osier willows were harvested from the island by basket makers. Volunteers today still harvest the willows for basket making demonstrations in the local area. They're also passionate about preserving rare local wildlife and maintaining the wilderness of the island. Volunteers deal with the range of items that wash up on the island, ranging from coconuts to polo balls! The last wooden barge on the River Thames is now rotting by the side of the island. There are also a couple of houseboats moored to the island today.

Size and location:
Approximate size: 40,467m²
Coordinates: 51.468, -0.321

Can you visit?
No, it's a protected nature reserve, but you can visit if you join one of the London Wildlife Trust's volunteering days (www.wildlondon.org.uk).

Carl's tips:
Town Wharf (Swan Street, TW7 6RJ) and the London Apprentice (62 Church Street, TW7 6BG) pubs both offer views of Isleworth Ait from the outdoor seating areas.

100 m/328 ft

High Street

Mortlak

Flowerpot Islands

These two tiny wooded islands used to be one island, but the Duke of Queensbury ordered it to be divided into two in the 18th century. Erosion caused them to shrink in size, although they've been protected from disappearing completely by measures taken by the local authorities.

Size and location:
Approximate size: 450m² each
Coordinates: 51.459, -0.311

Can you visit?
No.

Carl's tips:
Get a closer look by hiring a rowing skiff from Richmond Bridge Boathouses (www.richmondbridgeboathouses.co.uk), but you're not allowed to moor onto the islands.

Kingston Vale

20 m/66 ft

gston Vale

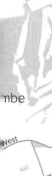

nbe

West

Corporation Island

This heavily wooded island is near Richmond Bridge and overlooks Richmond's riverfront, one of the most sought-after areas in Greater London. It was named Corporation Island to celebrate Richmond becoming a borough in the 19th century. Not many people know that this is the location of the penultimate photoshoot of The Beatles in 1969. The four of them were pictured rowing the Fritz Otto Maria Anna boat to the island and waving to the photographers on the mainland. Nowadays, this uninhabited island just has a few decaying boats lining its shores.

Size and location:
Approximate size: 6,772m²
Coordinates: 51.458, -0.309

Can you visit?
Yes, access by boat only.

Carl's tips:
Take in the island from a boat or skiff, or simply get a great view of it from the buzzing Richmond riverside. There are a couple of riverfront cafés with outdoor seating, ideal for watching the river life passing by.

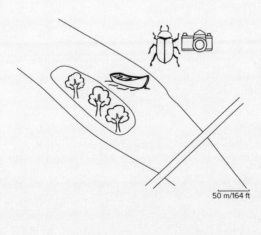

50 m/164 ft

CORPORATION ISLAND

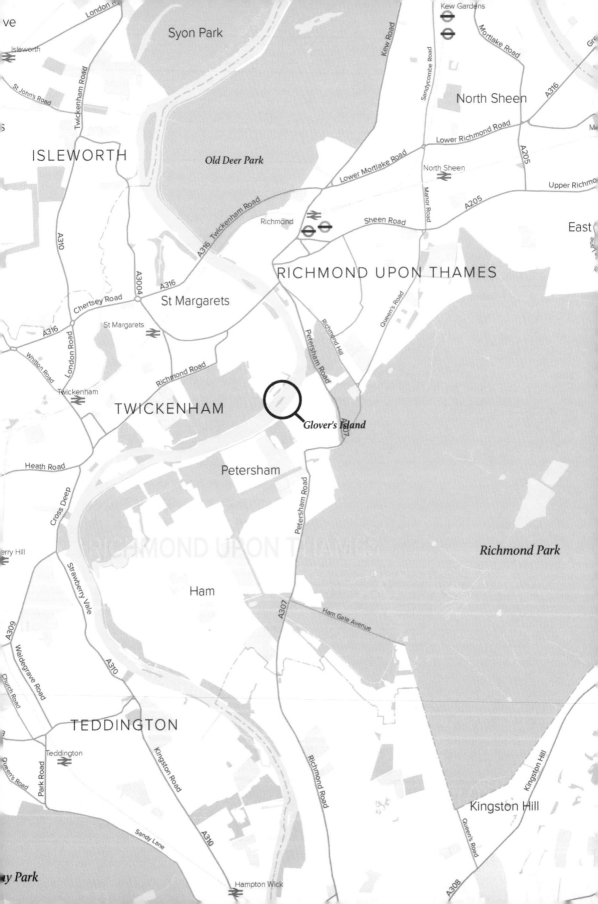

High Street

Mortlal

Glover's Island

This island was originally bought by a Richmond waterman called Joseph Glover in 1872. He bought it for just £70. Found in one of London's most exclusive districts, it would certainly be worth significantly more nowadays. Glover built a boathouse, workshop, dry dock and garden on the island, only the remnants of which are visible today. After a couple of decades, Glover was struggling to sell the island and tried to persuade the local council to buy it, bizarrely threatening to otherwise sell it to Pears Soap Company so they could erect a large advertising board. The council wasn't tempted at the time, although the island did eventually fall into their possession. The uninhabited island is particularly high because rubble from the London Underground excavation was dumped on it in the 19th century. Nowadays the island is very heavily wooded. Glover's Island forms the centre of the postcard-perfect view from Richmond Hill, which is the only view in England to be protected by an Act of Parliament.

Size and location:
Approximate size: 5,530m²
Coordinates: 51.450, -0.306

Can you visit?
Yes, access by boat only, although steep concrete shedding makes it difficult to land.

Carl's tips:
Drinking in that amazing view of Glover's Island from Richmond Hill is an absolute must. Afterwards, pop into The Roebuck pub (130 Richmond Hill, TW10 6RN) for a drink or pub lunch. You can also walk alongside the island on a pristine stretch of the River Thames towpath on the Richmond side. Afterwards, head over to the ever-popular Petersham Nurseries (Church Lane, Petersham Road, TW10 7AB), for a cup of tea in the sprawling garden and greenhouse of this high-end garden centre.

Kingston Vale

ston Vale

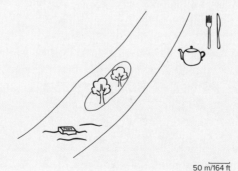

50 m/164 ft

be

est

Trap

GLOVER'S ISLAND

High Street
Mortlak
Kingston Vale
ston Vale
be
est
Trap

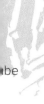

Eel Pie Island

This is the most famous island on the River Thames with a colourful history involving music legends, alternative lifestyles and all things creative. Accessible by footbridge or boat, this inhabited island has a vibrant rhythm of life, in-keeping with the many stories from its past. Indeed, the island has a long history, with evidence of ancient human settlements in the form of flints and axes, that have been dated back to at least 10,000BC. Although the island had other names in the past – as have many of the other River Thames islands – its Eel Pie Island name is due to the reportedly delicious eel pies previously served there.

In the 19th century, the Eel Pie Island Hotel was built, making the island a holiday spot, particularly for Londoners wishing to get out of the city. In the early 1900s, some wooden chalets were built on the island, reportedly to house the mistresses of local businessmen. A local antiques dealer called Michael Snapper bought the Eel Pie Hotel in 1951 and this marks the beginning of the island becoming legendary for music. The Eel Pie Island Hotel and its Eelpiland Jazz Club became a major jazz and blues venue throughout the 1950s and 60s. The Rolling Stones, David Bowie, Eric Clapton and Pink Floyd all played there. Rod Stewart's career is also said to have started on the island.

The hotel closed in the late 1960s due to disrepair and complaints about the hedonistic behaviour it brought to the island. It was reopened a short time later by Caldwell Smythe from The Riot Squad, under the new name of Colonel Barefoot's Rock Garden. Black Sabbath, Genesis, The Who and Deep Purple all went on to perform there. Pete Townshend from The Who later named his publishing company, Eel Pie Publishing, after the island. He also owns Eel Pie Studios on the mainland near the island, which is the site of many significant pop and rock recordings.

In 1969, the Eel Pie Island Hotel was occupied by a group of anarchists, including the illustrator Clifford Harper. By 1970, it was the largest hippie commune in the UK, called the Eel Pie Island Commune. After more than 140 years, a fire led to the eventual demolition of the legendary hotel.

The island has grown into a community of artists and boat workers, with around 50 houses, 120 inhabitants and a few houseboat moorings. The island still keeps its sense of anarchic creativity. In a 2005 TV show, *How to Start Your Own Country*, presenter Danny Wallace claimed to be the leader of Eel Pie Island, saying he had invaded it after crossing the footbridge. After a few hours, the police forced him to give the island back peacefully to the Queen.

In another unexpected turn, the island's boatyard also offers a boat service for Hindus and Sikhs to scatter the ashes of their loved ones in the river. The popularity of this service means the River Thames has been named by some as an honorary tributary of the River Ganges.

Nowadays, a single path passes through the centre of the island, with homes on either side of it. The Aquarius development of townhouses is on the site of the former Eel Pie Island Hotel. Near the boatyard is a row of artist studios, which host open weekends for the public a few times a year (www.eelpieislandartists.co.uk). Richmond Yacht Club (www.richmondyachtclub.co.uk) and Twickenham Rowing Club (www.twickenhamrc.co.uk) are also based on the island; the latter is one of the oldest rowing clubs on the river. Various public figures live or have lived on the island, including the original Doctor Who actor William Hartnell and the inventor, Trevor Baylis OBE CBE.

Size and location:
Approximate size: 44,250m²
Coordinates: 51.446, -0.324

Can you visit?
In theory the island is private, accessible only to inhabitants and the island's workers. However, many islanders encourage curious visitors to have a look.

Carl's tips:
Visit the island during the Eel Pie Island Artists Open Studios or for a Richmond Yacht Club social event. The Barmy Arms (The Embankment, TW1 3DU) old-school pub has a view of the island too. For an amazing insight into the many stories – past and present – about Eel Pie Island, visit the Eel Pie Island Museum (1-3 Richmond Road, TW1 3AB; www. eelpiemuseum.co.uk) in central Twickenham.

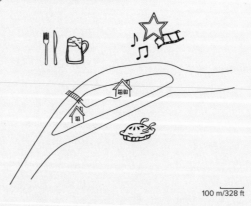

100 m/328 ft

EEL PIE ISLAND

In loving memory of

Trevor Baylis OBE CBE
Inventor

As the man who invented the wind-up radio, Trevor helped bring education about HIV/AIDS to Africa. His invention was endorsed by Nelson Mandela, and he has been awarded Officer and Commander of the Most Excellent Order of the British Empire (OBE, CBE) for his work.

How did you come to live on Eel Pie Island?

I grew up during the war in Southall in the west of London. My parents were also my teachers, since the bombs were coming down and the schools were closed. My mother was an artist, a thespian and a potter and my father taught me to use a Meccano set: I was an engineer by the age of six! Swimming was my first love – I used to swim for Great Britain – and I combined this with engineering to form my own swimming pool company. My connection to Eel Pie Island began with traditional jazz. I went to all the jazz clubs across London, which included the jazz club at the Eel Pie Island Hotel, where the Aquarius development is now. All the famous names in music went to Eel Pie Island, and I just loved the area and the community. I did my National Service, became a physical training instructor in the army and then I was invited to do an underwater escape act with a big sarcophagus for the Berlin Circus in 1970. They paid very well and I earned enough money to be able to buy a plot of land on Eel Pie Island.

Tell us about your house.

It's the house of my dreams: I built it myself. I got as far as the damp proof course and realised that bricklaying is a real skill, so I got friends to do that, but I did the rest. I built an indoor swimming pool and due to the changing river levels, I added the soil from this to the back of the house to make a flood barrier. So if there's a mayday situation, it won't all go bang! And of course I built a workshop for all my boy's toys. Building my house is the best thing I've ever done. Outside I have upper and lower levels with lazy lawns and vinyl flowers so I don't have to do any gardening! On the lower level I have a hot tub and a 1920s style car I made from scratch with a full Cortina engine in it. It's called TGB, for Trevor Graham Baylis. My view is just of water and trees – it's like being in the middle of the countryside. I called my home 'The Haven' as it's a place where I can put my feet up and chill out.

Describe the island's location.

It definitely feels like an island, but it's easy to get across to the mainland via the bridge. The location is fantastic – just five minutes' walk away from all the shops and restaurants of Twickenham. The island is 10 minutes from the railway station, then it only takes 20 minutes on the fast train to central London. Many people walk across the bridge onto Eel Pie Island and admire the view – it's better than Hyde Park. The only noise you get is from the occasional aircraft, depending on which way the wind's blowing. Even when the rugby is on, there are thousands of people in Twickenham, but you wouldn't know it from Eel Pie Island. It's like Brighton in the middle of London.

Describe the community on Eel Pie Island.

We're a family. It's a very tight community and we're all very hands on in our work, driven by achievement rather than money. There are artists, painters, potters and engineers like myself. A lot of us have boats, so we can trawl down the river and take it all in. What's so nice is that we come and go to each other's houses – if someone wants to pop in and use the lathe in my workshop or make me a cup of tea, they are welcome! I like the fact the island is not full of snobs. And I know that if I suddenly have a problem, my neighbours would be here to help me. We have regular social events and get togethers at Richmond Yacht Club on the island for music, fish and chips or just drinks. What the hell else do you want in life?

You've met royalty, world leaders and famous public figures. Who are the most memorable people you've spent time with?

I've met the most extraordinary people. I raised money for the Mines Advisory Group by walking 100 miles across the Namib Desert, and I met Princess Diana, who was the patron. She was a wonderful woman; she gave me a pith helmet as a present that I still keep on display in my house today. In the desert, I wore my electric shoe invention, which charges a mobile phone as you walk. I actually phoned Richard Branson from the desert using my shoe! Virgin had turned down my radio idea before, but this time Richard said I should come and meet him when I was back from Namibia. Nelson Mandela invited me to spend two days with him in Pretoria after I invented the wind-up radio. We also went to Buckingham Palace together several times, for meals and parties. We were like a couple of old buddies and I was so grateful to call him a friend. Soon I'll be meeting Catherine, Duchess of Cambridge, which I'm looking forward to. It's a great honour and weird; I'm just an ordinary bloke.

Tell us about your wind-up radio invention.
I don't get up in the morning saying I'm going to invent something – it doesn't work like that. In this case, I was watching a television programme about the spread of HIV/AIDS in Africa. I could have been watching anything, but it happened to be that. The programme said the only way they could do something about the disease was through education, which could be brought to people using the radio. But most of Africa didn't have electricity and batteries were horrendously expensive. I went to my workshop, got a DC motor and joined two wires to the back of a cheap transistor, wound it up and got sound. I'd done all this within half an hour of watching the programme.

What's your ethos on having a fulfilling life?
My mum was very clear in her advice to me: she told me to have a life. I like the saying: 'there are no pockets in a shroud' – your worldly wealth can't be kept and used after death. The thought of putting on a suit and a Rolex watch every day to commute into London never appealed to me. Is that a life? It's not about money – you can only wear one suit at a time and you won't be remembered for your Rolex watch. I knew a city worker once who died at 42 and left his multi-million pound fortune to the local cats home. Why didn't he just work at the cats home? I'm just very grateful to have what I've got and to be where I am.

What is your life philosophy?
Achievement is more important than qualifications. Society has been really kind to me – I've been awarded 11 PhDs, four Master's and a few professorships. But it's a bit ridiculous! There's no point being a master chef if you can't fry an egg.

What's your message to the next generation of inventors?
We're all inventors. I don't want people to think you have to have a Viennese accent, broken glasses and a brain like Einstein to be an inventor. I'm very anti-*Dragon's Den*; it shouldn't be a game show. Someone might have a great idea, but they could be camera shy or not very articulate. I'm trying to get invention into schools via the national curriculum. Sometimes it's the simplest of things that change our lives socially and commercially. The Romans invented the toilet for example; now we take this for granted.

What do you want to be remembered for?
I'm proud of my wind-up clock, torch and other inventions because they helped to bring about change. But I want to be remembered for helping people. I'm working with the Metropolitan Police and British Standards to help ensure ideas aren't stolen. The theft of intellectual property should become a white collar crime. Think about paper clips, for example. If we knew who created them, they would have made billions out of it. These are the things I'd like to leave behind – protecting inventors and making it possible for them to bring their ideas to market.

What do you like to do in your spare time?

I take my Jaguar E-Type for a drive. The engineering is brilliant and it's incredible how those old cars have gone up in value. I like joking with people by saying: 'I can only afford an old car!'

What's the best thing about living on Eel Pie Island?

The British Council took me all around the world and I had some extraordinary experiences, but sometimes I just missed home. I called my home 'The Haven' because that's exactly what it is.

Trevor Baylis passed away a few months after we met him for this interview. A man with incredible wit, charm and unshakeable positivity – who did so much for the world – we're honoured to publish one of his last ever interviews.

EEL PIE ISLAND

Michele Whitby
Eel Pie Island book author and museum curator

An author, houseboat dweller and driving force behind the Eel Pie Island Museum, Michele has had a connection with the island for decades.

How did you first discover Eel Pie Island?

I grew up in the local area, but I didn't visit Eel Pie Island until I was 21. Before that, it was just a vague part of the riverside vista. After college, two of my graphic designer friends got a studio on the island. Within a week of visiting them, I'd set up my own studio space on the island too! Eel Pie Island got under my skin then and it's been a part of me ever since.

Describe the creative landscape on the island in those days.

From the late 1980s, there were lots of small, affordable spaces for creatives at the boatyard. There was a great mix of people working on the boats, as well as many artistic craftspeople, including photographers, jewellers, blacksmiths, glassworkers, carpenters and people working with textiles. Someone once commented that you could commission a house to be built, fitted and furnished with all the skills that were here. It was a buzzing, vibrant place. A fire in 1996 destroyed much of this creative, chaotic part of the island. Nowadays, there are a just few artist studios left, which are very precious spaces.

Tell us about your work.

I had a photographic studio on the island to start with, but I've had a number of workshop spaces both on the island and elsewhere over the years. After photography I went back to my original passion, which was textiles. I did leather work, making really upmarket baseball caps out of suede and leather, which I sold to Harrods and other places.

Why did you decide to write a book about Eel Pie Island?

When I first came to the island, my parents and their friends told me about all these huge names in music who had played there. I wondered why no one had written a book about the island; it just seemed like the most exciting piece of rock and roll history. I think it took

someone a generation removed from it to see how significant it was. It became a backburner project I researched in between having kids, running a shop and various other projects.

How did your book come into fruition?

Stories and photos came flooding in when I put out some feelers. Through another connection I met the former manager of Eel Pie music club, Arthur Chisnall. I became really good friends with him over a number of years and gathered lots of information from him. I also heard that another islander, Dan van der Vat, was researching a book. He's written a lot of historical publications, so collaborating with him worked really well; I did the music history and he did the rest. We approached a publisher, they said yes very quickly, and within around six months of signing the contract, our book was on the shelves.

Then you took everything a step further to create the Eel Pie Island Museum?

At the time the book was released I still had my own shop selling locally made arts and crafts. It seemed natural to have the book launch there, which I did alongside an exhibition of old Eel Pie Island photos and memorabilia that I had collected. I realised how special and important it was in terms of local heritage, which was the first seed of an idea for a museum. A few years later, I curated an exhibition at Orleans House Stables Gallery about Eel Pie Island's musical past. It was part of a larger project which also included a film and book, The British Beat Explosion: Rock 'N' Roll Island, which I contributed a chapter to. It was the most successful exhibition they'd ever had, with unprecedented visitor numbers. So many people said it should be permanent, which felt like another endorsement that a museum was a good idea. The first version of the Eel Pie Island Museum was a five month pop-up at Twickenham Library. I had to raise all the funding for it as well as organise the exhibits: it was a substantial and quite stressful project. And then I embarked on a bigger and even more stressful project: the permanent Eel Pie Island Museum! Thankfully I have a great team of volunteers helping me, without whom I simply couldn't do it.

Tell us about the museum.

It's divided into the four main areas the island is known for: music heritage, invention, historical boatyards and creativity. Each one is a huge subject in itself. Music is obviously what made the island famous, but this subject alone covers traditional jazz, skiffle, British Blues, psychedelic sounds, progressive rock and the beginnings of heavy metal. The museum has a roll call of the dates musicians played on the island. One woman brought her diary from 1964 to the pop-up museum to show me John Lee Hooker played on a particular day. Another lovely lady visited me with her daughter to donate a fantastic painting her late husband had done of the island when he was 19. So I've pieced together information from many sources! The Rolling Stones even signed a special photo-montage that I made of them playing here back in the 60s. I'm really passionate about all the boatyard history too, so that's an important aspect of the museum. The Thames is a huge artery of London, but boatyards are being eroded and replaced with apartments. We've also recreated Trevor Baylis's workshop in the museum. There's so much more information constantly coming in that we'll be able to keep the exhibits fresh for a long time to come.

Is there anything unexpected you uncovered in your research?

I found out that Daimler motor company tested some of their early petrol engines on the island, because they weren't allowed to test them on the roads. I previously had no idea some of the beginnings of the car industry happened on Eel Pie Island. For me personally, I was most excited when I found out David Bowie had played on the island. I'm a massive Bowie fan and couldn't believe he'd walked down the same path I walk along every day!

What will be your lasting impression of creating the Eel Pie Island Museum?

Eel Pie has got many tethers that go out all over the world; it's a really special place to so many people. There's something remarkable about gathering together their stories and memories. It will never cease to amaze me how the island has touched so many people.

Describe where you live on the island.

I've lived on a houseboat moored to Eel Pie Island since the early 2000s. I rent the boat from my friend of 25 years; I've got pictures of us partying on the boat when we were much younger! The island and the boat have always been part of my adult life in one form or another. My boyfriend lives on a big boat next door, so we basically have a double house with a pontoon in between. We have a million pound view: it's gorgeous during every season of the year.

What do you like about houseboat living?

I'm a keen swimmer, so being on the water seems really natural to me. I don't think I'd live on land again. There's something special about that gentle rock of the water as you're falling asleep. I also love the sound of activity from the boatyard, of people hammering and welding, or boats being craned in and out. It's not a lifestyle that would suit everyone. For example, you have to keep an eye on your fuel supply for the wood burning stove in winter; you can't just turn the central heating on. I quite like the act of getting the wood and chopping it up. By the time you've done that, it's warmed you up anyway, so you don't need the fire on anymore! Before this I had a four-storey property: a basement, my shop and two floors of living space. Within six months I cleared out everything I didn't need so I could live on the houseboat; it was a liberating process.

Describe the feeling on Eel Pie Island.

As soon as I get to the top of the footbridge and then start walking onto the island, a feeling of contentment washes over me. It's a combination of being away from the mainland, having the peace of no cars and knowing all the islanders. It can easily take half an hour to get on and off the island because you stop and chat to everyone. I love the social side of it and it feels like a big family, even though people are from very different backgrounds with different degrees of wealth. Everyone just gets on. We're all quirky in some way too. Lots of the people love boats or the river. One of the residents says that you either come here and move off after a year because it's not for you, or you come here and you only leave in a wooden box.

Are there social get-togethers on the island?

Richmond Yacht Club on the island has little social events and activities like film clubs and yoga. There's always something going on somewhere. Get-togethers are often impromptu. I popped over to the house of my caricaturist friends, Simon and Sheba, one afternoon for a meeting about a business collaboration. I didn't leave until the early hours of the morning! If you live on Eel Pie Island, you'll have a random evening with various people sooner or later, where conversation and wine is flowing. It's probably not good for your liver, but it's definitely good for your soul!

Why has Eel Pie Island got such a creative atmosphere?

I think part of the reason the music scene sprung up on the island was because there was freedom to make more noise than you could on the mainland. The history has probably helped creativity prevail today. Quite a few people have told me Eel Pie Island is on a ley line. I'm not massively into that kind of thing, but there's definitely a special energy to the place. There's something that keeps people coming back.

What's the most unexpected thing about island life?

When the tide is very high, the bottom of the footbridge gets cut off. In the summer; we just walk through the water. But in the winter, we have to take our boots off and wade through icy cold water, or some people wrap bin bags over their shoes. Sometimes we just stand there chatting until the bottom of the bridge appears again. It would seem like a real inconvenience to some, but to us it's just part of island life. My daughter was late for school once because the tide was up; it was the first time her teacher had heard that particular excuse!

Henry and Blaine Harrison
Mystery Jets

Father and son Henry and Blaine are two of the founders of the Mystery Jets indie rock band. The band have played the British Summertime Festival, Latitude Festival and were the last band to play at the London Astoria before it was demolished. Their headquarters is on Eel Pie Island.

How did the Mystery Jets begin?

Henry: I'm an architect, but I love music, especially progressive rock. When Blaine and his best friend William were eight years old, I got them into Pink Floyd, King Crimson and Yes. They were planning a band together by the age of 10. We initially called ourselves the Misery Jets because of the noise from the flight path over Richmond, where I was living. Blaine was living in France with his mother at the time and through our letters and drawings to each other, the name evolved to Mystery Jets. William and I visited Blaine in France regularly and we wrote music and played gigs.

Blaine: I was living in quite an isolated part of France, so I became aware of the universal language of music at a young age. Music provided me with a connection to home and to my dad, who gave me Pink Floyd's *Dark Side of the Moon* on my eighth birthday. That was my lightbulb moment. Very soon after I got a drum kit and William got a guitar. Our early stuff sounded absolutely dreadful – thankfully very few recordings still exist.

What brought you to Eel Pie Island?

Henry: I'd always wanted to live on the island, mainly because of its musical history and special atmosphere. I bought some land after the boatyard burned down in 1996. It was a difficult situation: around 60 artists lost their studios and work in the fire. It took a good few years to clear the space and build Phoenix Wharf, which would eventually become my home as well as providing spaces for creative design studios and a boatyard.

Describe your Eel Pie Island HQ.

Henry: Blaine and I write lyrics together regularly at Phoenix Wharf. We've got a small recording studio and the space is littered with our own artwork, posters, relics and all kinds of memorabilia. We're great Pink Floyd fans and we bought some of Syd Barrett's furniture when he died. I always see everything about Mystery Jets as being connected to the island. We recorded the first album here which incorporates the island sounds.

Blaine: It's the spiritual HQ of the band. When we first came to Eel Pie Island, there was a bit of resistance to a bunch of kids making a racket in a portacabin. We were told to shut up and turn it down quite a lot. I think the island has taken us into its embrace over the years. We're on the road a lot, but we have a feeling of coming home when we're on Eel Pie Island.

Where do you find inspiration?

Blaine: Eel Pie Island is such an inspiration. The artist studios have open weekends in the summer. It feels like a utopian world and it revives your hope in things. It's wonderful that in one of the biggest cities in the world, there's a place where people can escape into themselves and create work. I also love the boats. They make a very peaceful sound at night, quietly knocking against one another. We lived on a narrowboat for many years while Phoenix Wharf was being built. I'd wake up in the morning and listen to the world passing by on the river. Everything slows down when you're next to the water. Time becomes elastic and you feel anything's possible.

Henry: We spent three years writing our *Curve of the Earth* album and wrote a lot of the lyrics on Eel Pie Island.

How did you transition from music as a hobby to a career?

Blaine: After I moved back to the UK, we had our first experiences in a recording studio. We booked our first tour the year William and I left school, playing up and down the country to lots of empty rooms! The joy of being on stage was enough to keep us hooked. William and I went to art school, but deep down we knew music was our future.

Henry: We started getting a name for ourselves around the early 2000s, after playing gigs in all the right places in Camden and Islington. We recorded two EPs of our early music and sent them to NME. They thought it was weird and interesting that a 14 year old kid was singing these complex lyrics. Then we met our future manager and played to three major labels on Eel Pie Island. There ended up being a bidding war!

You've supported bands including Arctic Monkeys, Mumford & Sons and The Maccabees. You've also done the British Summertime Festival, Latitude Festival and you played the last gig at the London Astoria before it was demolished. What's next?

Henry: It would be ideal to tour the world in our own right. Blaine lives for touring especially. It's tough to find sustainability in the music industry and a lot of good bands have gone because they couldn't make it work. We run a very tight ship: if we're not touring, we're writing. It's a massive discipline. You must have faith in what you're doing and you must believe that you're stepping up this musical ladder.

Blaine: It's an interesting time in music; there are no apparent rules to be followed or to be broken. I want to allow people to project themselves onto our music, which comes from not explaining the songs and allowing people to come to it themselves. When I listened to *Dark Side of the Moon* as a child, I had no idea it was about consumerism, money and politics, but I was able to create my own worlds within that soundtrack. That's what we aspire to do with our music.

Henry was voted NME's 18th coolest man in rock and the two of you were nominees for the Ivor Novello Awards. How does it feel to get recognition from all different angles?

Henry: I think awards are good to get some kind of recognition. It's a big deal for bands to be nominated for awards, where you're judged by fellow songwriters in particular. Blaine also enjoys going on music programmes, talking about other people's music, like the BBC Radio Six Music Roundtable. These are all stepping stones to the band being heard as far afield as possible.

Blaine has spina bifida and is one of the patrons for the charity, Attitude is Everything. What influence do you hope to have on the music industry's stance towards disabilities?

Blaine: The music industry needs to take more notice of disabled music lovers. Experiencing the power of music in a crowd is absolutely euphoric. Working with Attitude is Everything is about educating the industry about how even small changes can enable live music to be more open and accessible. There's a huge proportion of people who could be coming to shows and paying for tickets who simply haven't been taken into consideration. It's something I feel very passionate about.

Describe Eel Pie Island.

Henry: It's the most gorgeous island. There's a quiet part, a nature reserve at each end and a lively part, where we are. The magic of the island is being here at dawn and dusk, when life wakes up and closes down. The island belongs equally to people and nature. You feel the vibrancy and the island unfolds as you walk along the path. This stretch of the Thames is very lively for boat life too. I like looking out and seeing activity, not just blank water.

Blaine: The island feels like a refuge. When you walk over the footbridge, the city becomes quietened. My first impression was that I was stepping into an Enid Blyton novel. You're in the hustle and bustle of London one minute, then you cross the river to another world. That really appealed to us as musicians, because with our music, we wanted to take people to a place where anything was possible. That's what great music does and the island gave us a platform to do that.

What kind of people does Eel Pie Island attract?

Blaine: There's something about being on an island and surrounded by water that allows you a certain headspace, which is very appealing to creatively minded people.

Henry: It doesn't attract uncreative people. Island living is an alternative lifestyle and very unconventional. We've got hi-tech and internet savvy people and we're surrounded by artist studios, the boating community and a bohemian way of life. I like the idea of there being a connection between all the people living and working on the island, forming networks. In central London, you might be working next to creative people, but you just haven't got the time to connect with them. And of course we've got Trevor Baylis, the island's icon.

What advice would you give someone hoping to live on an island?

Henry: Living on an island is incredibly inconvenient. Whenever you go to the mainland, you have to remember to do all your errands because getting on and off the island takes time. Islands are like villages from the Middle Ages: everyone knows each other and there's no real privacy. But the joy of it is being surrounded by water and feeling the magic of the place.

Blaine: This part of the Thames is tidal, so my advice is not to wear your fresh sneakers or your skinny jeans when you come to visit. Once the island works its charms on you, you won't be leaving in a hurry... and you may well have to wade your way back to your car.

What has been your most momentous occasion on the island?

Henry: We hosted a series of parties between 2003 and 2005. We wanted to start our own west London music scene, a bit like The Libertines east London scene. It took off incredibly well: we started with a small group of friends and ended up with about 900 people trying to get into a small room to hear 10 bands play.

Blaine: Word spread very quickly and we had no idea how many people would turn up to each one. People felt the allure of crossing the water. They found an appeal in not being watched and doing whatever they liked. It must have been a similar feeling to when the hotel used to be a popular spot. We didn't charge any money nor run a bar; we just told people to come and watch music, bring their own drinks and hang out. After a while, newspapers and talent scouts turned up too.

Why did your Eel Pie parties end?

Blaine: We were served a noise abatement order of £20,000! I think it gave us the ultimatum that we secretly, subconsciously felt we needed. The parties had outgrown what we'd originally intended to do.

Henry: We went out in style! I think we revived the spirit of the island that was here in the 1960s and I feel proud we did that.

Swan Island

The first of two islands on the Thames named Swan Island, this island is connected to the mainland by a road bridge. The island used to be a small mudflat which was built up at the end of the 19th century using clay derived from the building of the London Underground. The island itself today is a boatyard, while attached to its banks is a thriving community of houseboats.

Size and location:
Approximate size: 2,000m²
Coordinates: 51.439, -0.331

Can you visit?
Yes, just walk over the bridge.

Carl's tips:
Get a view of the island from Radnor Gardens just a stone's throw away on the mainland. There's a small kiosk for a coffee or cream tea pit stop too.

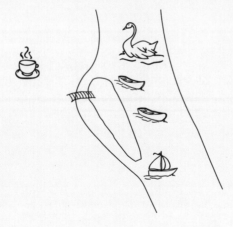

20 m/66 ft

Teddington Lock

This is the largest lock system of the River Thames, forming the boundary between the tidal and non-tidal stretches of the river. The long, functional island has some manicured lawns and can be accessed from the riverbank by a footbridge.

Size and location:
Approximate size: 6,000m²
Coordinates: 51.432, -0.325

Can you visit?
Yes, just walk over the footbridge.

Carl's tips:
Tide End Cottage (8 Ferry Road, TW11 9NN) is a pub nearby that celebrates this tidal and non-tidal junction of the river in its name. To walk almost exactly alongside the lock island, do so on the Thames Path in the wide green space of the Ham side of the river.

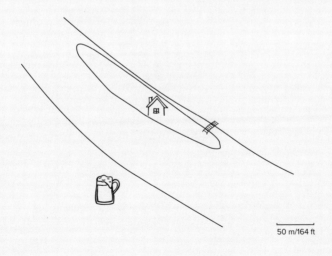

50 m/164 ft

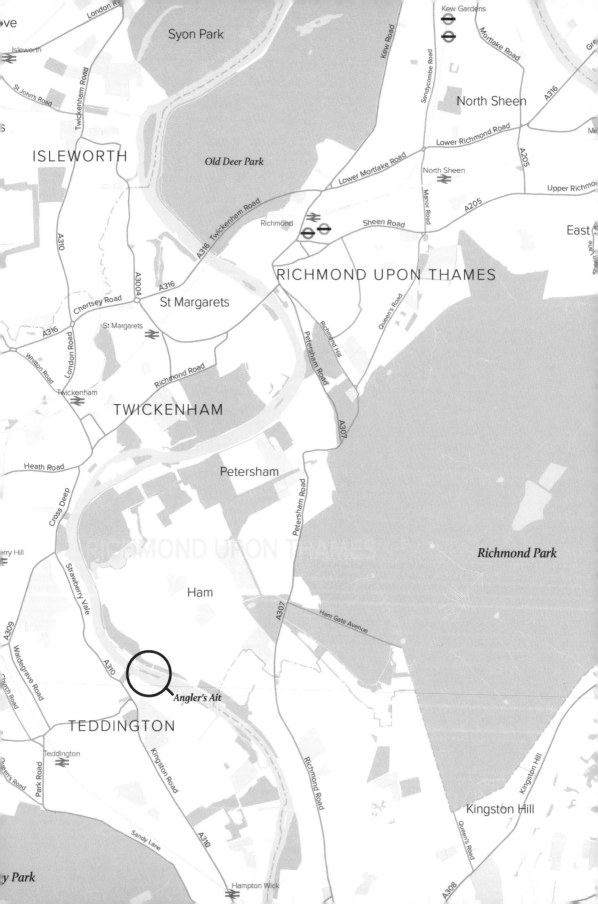

Angler's Ait

This skiff lock is named after the nearby pub, The Anglers. It's accessible via a footbridge from both riverbanks. The small island has lots of trees and a small shingle beach that gives you a close-up view of the water.

Size and location:
Approximate size: 4,200m²
Coordinates: 51.431, -0.322

Can you visit?
Yes, just walk over the footbridge.

Carl's tip:
Visit The Anglers pub (3 Broom Road, TW11 9NR), which has existed since the 18th century and was previously a popular drinking spot for local fishermen. There's a 3.5 mile circular walk on the iFootpath app (www.ifootpath.com) that starts and finishes at The Anglers, which also takes in Eel Pie Island and the many famous local landmarks.

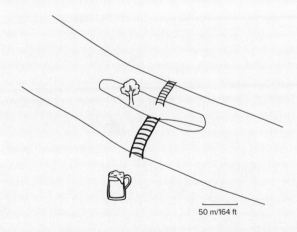

50 m/164 ft

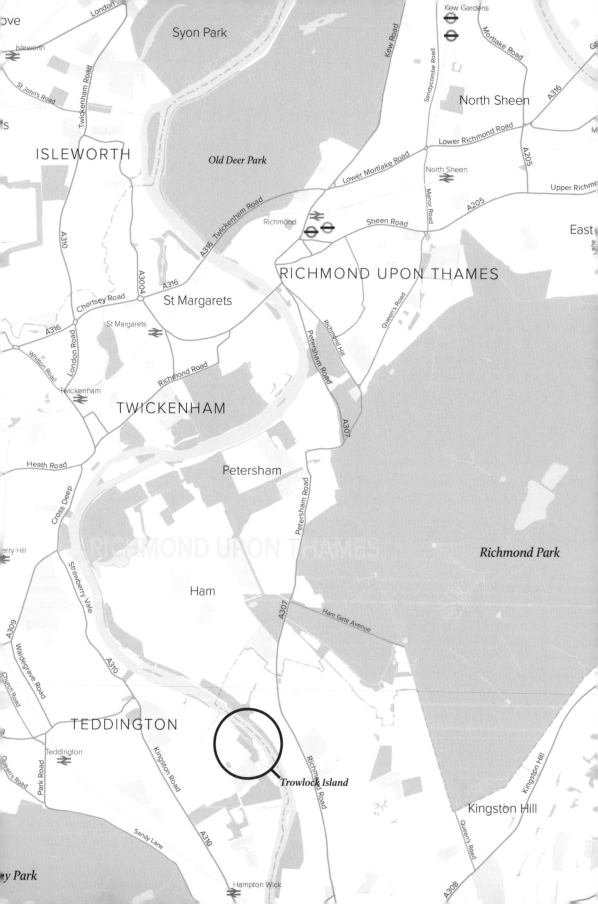

Trowlock Island

This is one of the River Thames islands that became a mini-break destination for Londoners during the late 19th century. Holidaymakers camped and stayed in wooden chalets during this time. The Royal Canoe Club also opened its clubhouse on the island during this era and the club is still based on the island today. Despite the fact the island floods intermittently, there are 29 residential bungalows on Trowlock Island, built on stilts to ward off flooding problems. There are also a few dozen houseboats moored to the island. Trowlock Island has a vibrant community spirit – there's a communal lawn, fire pit, barbecue and chairs specifically for the regular social events for islanders. Trowlock Island residents collectively own their island as it's run through a company called Trowlock Island Limited, which they're all shareholders in. Access to the island is via a charming old chain link ferry.

Size and location:
Approximate size: 16,000m²
Coordinates: 51.425, -0.310

Can you visit?
No, access is for residents only.

Carl's tips:
The best view of Trowlock Island is from the Ham side of the river, where the Thames Path passes through an area of lush greenery.

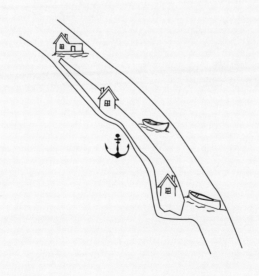

100 m/328 ft

Mary Newing
Holistic therapist and business trainer

This holistic therapist left the IT industry to pursue a portfolio career and a better work/life balance. Based on Trowlock Island, she's now a freelance IT trainer and a holistic therapist working in healing tents at festivals across the UK.

Why did you decide to live on Trowlock Island?

I was originally looking for somewhere to rent that would allow me to bring my beloved chinchillas with me. So I wasn't necessarily looking to live on an island, but I found the house on Trowlock Island and loved it. I moved in towards the end of the 1990s and eventually went on to buy the house I was renting. So the island has been home for a long time now.

Describe the feeling on Trowlock Island.

The island has a supportive and caring community. Trowlock Island residents mostly keep to themselves, but there are occasional social events we really enjoy too. The great thing is that I know I could ask my neighbours for help if I ever needed it. Living on the island connects me to nature and the rhythm of the seasons. I especially love being so close to nature in winter; the mist over the water on cold mornings is beautiful. I have to walk up the island and take the chain link ferry to get onto the mainland. This process in itself makes me more aware of seasonal changes and the environment around me.

What is the best thing about living on an island?

The island has houses on both sides with a path down the middle, so it's common to stop and chat with neighbours. Islanders come and go more than people living on a normal street, since getting on and off the island is an event in itself.

What advice would you give to someone thinking about living on an island?

Do it. It's lovely to be so close to the water and to have such a direct connection with nature.

Would you ever live on the mainland again?

I would, but I couldn't be too far from the water. If I had a house on the mainland, it would have to have its own mooring. I'd be really content living on a houseboat too.

What are the practicalities of living on an island like?

Trowlock Island does not have a bridge and can only be accessed by a chain link ferry. This means that only bicycles and barrows can come and go, so you have to carry everything from the car park to your house. Most of the time this is just fine, until you need to do a big supermarket shop. Most couriers will deliver to the island, but not surprisingly, it's very common for them to get lost or confused!

Steven's Eyot and Islet

The names of these islands have changed over the last couple of centuries, but Steven's Eyot – the name of a local boat maker – has stuck since the early 1900s. The smaller islet, home only to ducks and trees, makes way for the larger Steven's Eyot. This was the site of one of the first public swimming areas in the locality in the late 19th century. In the early 20th century, weekend picnickers would row to the island for some relaxation time. Since 1953, Steven's Eyot has been the home of the Small Boat Club (SBC). Members of the club travel there on their small boats or via the private ferry service at the weekends, to enjoy boating and social events.

Size and location:

Approximate size: 2,300m²
Coordinates: 51.420, -0.306

Can you visit?

No, access is for members of the SBC only.

Carl's tips:

Head to Canbury Gardens to see the island from the riverbank then have a drink at the locally loved pub, The Boaters Inn (Canbury Gardens, Lower Ham Road, KT2 5AU). Turks Launches (www.turks.co.uk) nearby runs river trips between Kingston and Hampton Court, where you can take in some of the islands along the way.

50 m/164 ft

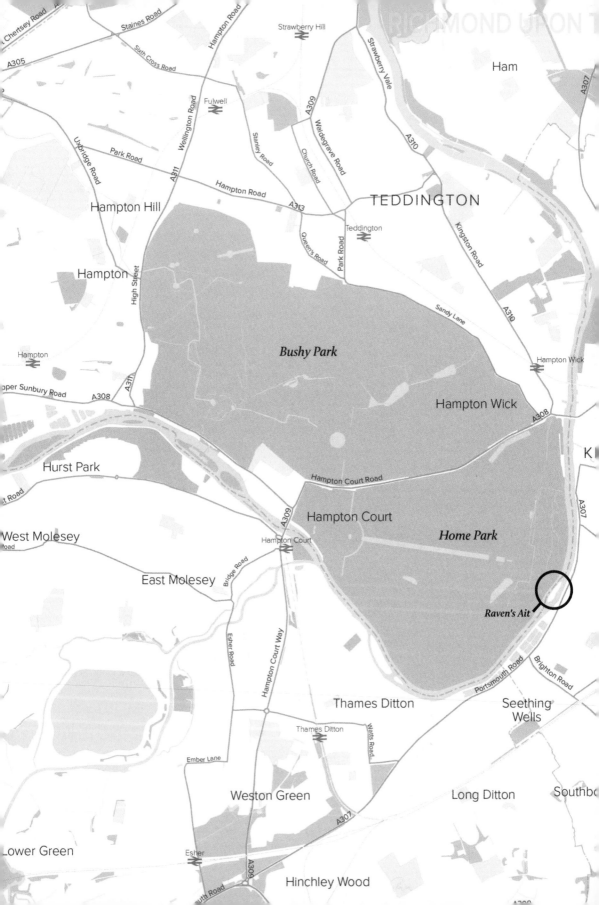

Raven's Ait

This island has a long and colourful history. Its most important claim to fame is as the site of the Treaty of Kingston, which saved England from submitting to French control in the 13th century. Comically, the island was named Raven's Arse for a stretch of time before it became an important rowing venue for Kingston Rowing Club in the 19th century, when the name changed to Raven's Ait. Hart's Boat Builders subsequently bought the island, then it went on to be leased by the Navy League. In the late 1980s, the local council bought the island after rumours emerged that the controversial media mogul, Robert Maxwell, was planning to buy it. In the years that followed, there was a dispute between locals and the council about whether the island was private or public land. In 2009, eco-protesters took over the island and opened it up to local people to enjoy, but they were eventually evicted. The leasehold of the island was eventually awarded to the sailing Olympian Ossie Stewart, who turned it into a venue available for weddings and public hire (www.ravensait.co.uk). It's now being run by an international businessman. During the summer, there is a thriving calendar of public events including open air cinema, beer festivals, barbecues and Sunday lunches.

Size and location:
Approximate size: 6,000m²
Coordinates: 51.399, -0.311

Can you visit?
Yes, catch the free ferry to the island's public events.

Carl's tips:
Get a great view of Raven's Ait from the Thames Path, which runs along the incredibly green Hampton Court side of the river. If you're on the more built-up Surbiton side, you can just about get a glimpse of Raven's Ait from the balconies of the high-end gastropub, The Hart's Boatyard (Portsmouth Road, KT6 4HL). If you want to get out on the water to see the local islands up close, hire a boat from Harts Cruisers (www.taggsboatyard.co.uk).

50 m/164 ft

Boyle Farm Island

This island is named after the Boyle Farm mansion on the riverbank, owned by the first Lord Saint Leonards in the 19th century. Lord Saint Leonards was a notable jurist, barrister and the Lord Chancellor. Boyle Farm Island today has a single cottage, secluded by trees. In 2015, a portion of the island was put up for sale for £150,000.

Size and location:
Approximate size: 3,000m²
Coordinates: 51.393, -0.330

Can you visit?
No, this is a privately owned, residential island.

Carl's tips:
Get a great view of Boyle Farm Island from the Thames Path on the Hampton Court side of the river.

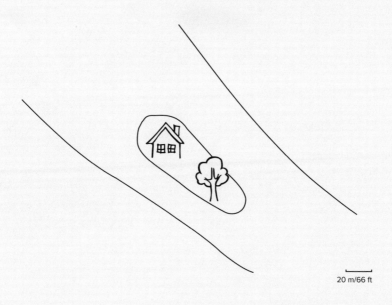

20 m/66 ft

Swan Island

A second island named Swan Island on the Thames, a local builder created Swan Island from clay excavated during the construction of the London Underground during the late 1890s. There was previously a modest ferryman's hut on the island, home to the man who transported people across the river to Hampton Court. The hut has been restored and updated in more recent years. A bridge of silt now connects the island to the much larger inhabited island next door: Thames Ditton Island.

Size and location:
Approximate size: 600m²
Coordinates: 51.393, -0.331

Can you visit?
No, this is a privately owned residential island.

Carl's tips:
Swan Island is barely distinguishable from Thames Ditton Island, but you have the best chance of seeing it from the Thames Ditton side of the river. The aptly named Ye Olde Swan pub (Summer Road, KT7 0QQ) is nearby, not far from the footbridge to Thames Ditton Island. And old the pub is too – an inn has been standing on this location since the 13th century. The pub used to own Thames Ditton Island too.

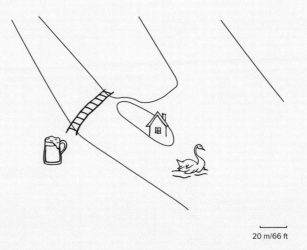

20 m/66 ft

Thames Ditton Island

This densely populated island has around 50 homes, many of which are on stilts, accessed by an elegant suspension footbridge. In the late 1800s, day tripping picnickers used to visit the island on skiffs, while holiday bungalows popped up across the island as it grew in popularity. In 1910, Maundy Gregory – a controversial figure – bought the bungalow called Vanity Fair on the island, which he shared with his platonic friend, the actress Edith Rosse. Gregory was a magazine publisher and property magnate, but he became known for blackmailing politicians and was suspected of murder on more than one occasion, including that of Rosse, who died in suspicious circumstances. Nowadays, Thames Ditton Island is known just as 'The Island' to its inhabitants. It's home to a vibrant community with pretty houses, a small public garden and fantastic views of Hampton Court Park. They're a sociable lot too, with annual duck race days, raft races, barbecues and Christmas get togethers.

Size and location:
Approximate size: 19,000m²
Coordinates: 51.394, -0.331

Can you visit?
No, only residents can access the island, but you can get a flavour of life on the island via the community website: www.thamesdittonisland.co.uk

Carl's tips:
A number of islanders enjoy Friday night drinks at Ye Olde Swan – another tick for this centuries' old pub. If you want to get out on the water to see the local islands up close, hire a boat from Ditton Cruisers (www.taggsboatyard.co.uk).

100 m/328 ft

Susie Morgan
Magazine editor

*After arriving on Thames Ditton Island by chance more than 20 years ago, Susie now works
at the heart of the local community.*

Why did you decide to live on an island?

I have lived on The Island at Thames Ditton since 1995. My partner played rugby professionally and his club rented a house for him, which just so happened to be on an island. We're still in the same house to this day. Back then it was a two-bedroom bungalow but we've since extended it into a three-bedroom family home for us and our two daughters.

Tell us about your work.

I'm the editor of Thames Ditton's community magazine, *About Thames Ditton*. Living on the island is perfect for this job. It's so close to the High Street, it means I can keep abreast of everything that's going. It's equally ideal to be aware of the side of Thames Ditton that happens on the water. The Thames is a big part of our village.

What kind of people does Thames Ditton Island attract?

The island attracts all sorts of people, including young families, retired couples and professional city workers. Many people love it so much they find it difficult to leave; my neighbour has lived in her house since 1954.

What is the worst thing about island living?

You have to be a certain kind of person to endure some of the downsides of island life, such as having to park some distance from your front door and the potential for high waters through wet spells. We always consider ourselves very lucky compared to some areas around the Thames which have flooded. Although we're surrounded by water, our homes don't get wet as they're all built so high up, usually on stilts.

What's the best thing about island living?

Most islanders own their own boats and we prefer to travel by boat if it's an option. It means you don't have to sit in traffic on the roads and it saves on parking. Christmas shopping moored up outside John Lewis in Kingston is much less stressful than getting in the car too!

Where's your favourite place off the island?

We just have to pop across the water to reach Home Park – Hampton Court's amazing grounds.

What feeling does living on the island give you?

I love the water, so watching and hearing the river moving always puts a smile on my face and makes me feel calm.

What advice would you give to other people interested in living on an island?

Choosing to live on an island gives you a lifestyle as well as a home. You either like it or you don't, but you become part of something amazing if you do like it. You also need to treat the river as an extension to your garden, which is perfect if you love the water like I do.

Would you ever leave Thames Ditton Island?

It's an addictive place to live. We've thought about moving numerous times, but the pull of island life and being on the water makes it very hard to leave. Having been here for so long already, I think we're here to stay.

Find out more about Susie's work at www.aboutthamesditton.co.uk

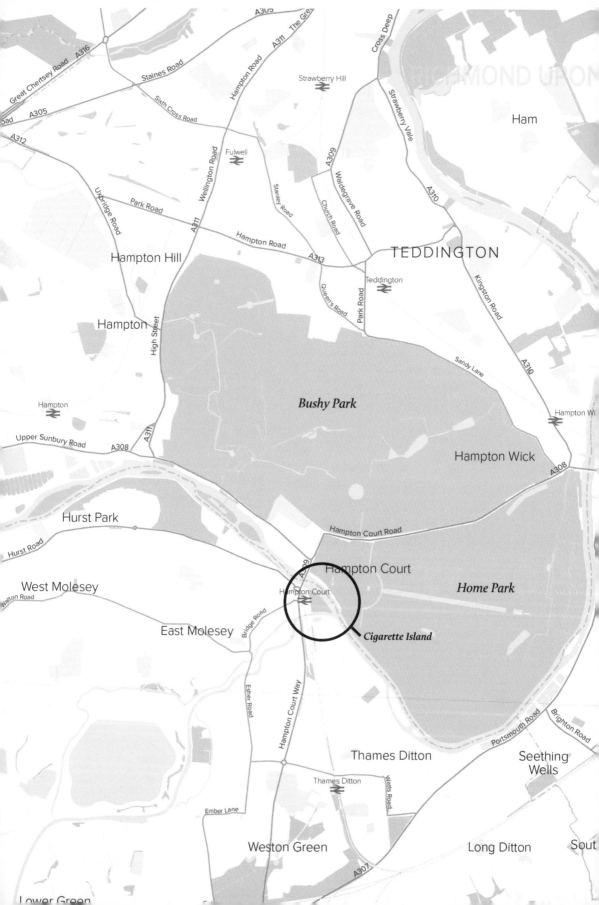

Cigarette Island

The riverbank across the river from Hampton Court Palace used to be an island, surrounded by the River Mole and River Thames. This was and still is the site of Hampton Court train station, which was previously accessed by bridges due to its island location. The name comes from a houseboat called Cigarette – owned by Member of Parliament Sir Henry Foreman – that was moored on the island during the 1920s. The Mole, which ran alongside Creek Road, was diverted in the 1930s, making the island disappear. The former island is now a park – Cigarette Island Park – while the railway station remains in the same spot.

Size and location:
Approximate size: 47,000m²
Coordinates: 51.402, -0.342

Can you visit?
Yes, no boat needed nowadays!

Carl's tips:
After checking out Cigarette Island Park, have a mooch along Bridge Road nearby for amazing antiques shops, pubs and pavement cafés. Then wander across Hampton Court Bridge for a few more shops and a visit to Hampton Court Palace itself. If you want to explore this stretch of the river by water, Martin Boats (Riverbank, KT8 9BH) has rowing boats available for hire by the hour. To avoid getting caught up in a lock system, only row downriver.

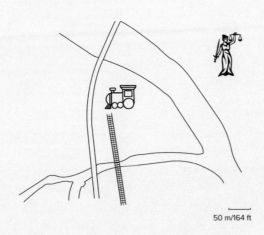

50 m/164 ft

Ash Island

This privately owned island has a boatyard, three houses and 50 houseboat moorings, which are home to approximately 80 people in total. The island is accessible by boat or via a footpath from Molesey Lock next door. Weirs at either end give islanders a constant background sound of crashing water. In the mid 1800s, the island was also home to a beer house, tea rooms and a skittle alley, but these eventually moved to neighbouring Taggs Island due to flooding.

Size and location:
Approximate size: 16,000m²
Coordinates: 51.407, -0.349

Can you visit?
No, only island residents or customers of the boatyard can go there.

Carl's tips:
The best view of Ash Island is from this beautiful stretch of the Thames Path, which runs along the Molesey side of the river.

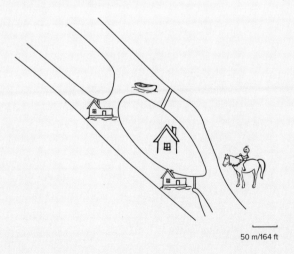

50 m/164 ft

ASH ISLAND

Suleman Akhtar

Boatyard owner

*With a family connection to Ash Island since he was a child, Suleman left his job
in the city to live and work on the island full time.*

When did you first discover Ash Island?

My grandfather was an apprentice boat builder in the 1930s and he worked in a large boatyard that used to be on the riverbank opposite Ash Island. He built boats there, including lifeboats during the early part of World War II, before he got called up to serve in the Far East. In 1969, he and my grandmother sold their six bedroom house in Esher and bought a houseboat on Ash Island. I can still vaguely remember my parents being quite shocked by that! Visiting them as a child was my first experience of the island.

Why did you decide to move to the island yourself?

My grandparents bought a house in the middle of the island in the 1970s, from an old couple called Mr and Mrs Booker. I still remember Mrs Booker – she lived on cigarettes and chocolate! My grandparents lived there until the early 2000s, when my grandmother died and my grandfather decided to move away. I was looking to buy a property at the time and I could either afford a tiny flat in Ealing, or a whole house on Ash Island. So I bought my grandfather out and have lived here ever since. My family and I own a large proportion of the island, so it's still very much a family affair. But I have no ambitions to take over the whole island!

Do you know the history of your house?

The chairman of Molesey Boat Club lived in the house from 1947 until the early 1960s. Whenever he wanted a bit of publicity for himself or the boat club, he used to make an anonymous phone call to the press to say there was an old man just about to ride his horse across the river. The press would turn up and then he would ride his horse, Tony, across from the boat club to Ash Island! There's a shed on the island we still call 'Tony's shed', where the horse was stabled. I've got old photos of the horse standing just outside where my kitchen door is now.

And now you own a business on the island too...

The boatyard T.W. Allen and Sons Ltd has operated on Ash Island since the 1920s, owned and run by the Allen family. They started out building wooden boats. When boats moved to fibreglass, they started a hire fleet instead. That crashed when the cheap package holidays of the 1970s came in. So they moved into providing residential houseboats, which is still the main focus of the business today. I bought the business from the family in 2008 and we still operate under the family name. There used to be 35 people working here but now there's just me. It's past its glory days, like most of British manufacturing. It's not a hugely commercial venture; I'm just happy as long as I earn enough to pay the mortgage and put some food on the table.

What did you do before becoming a boatyard owner?

I used to work in central London as an accountant, but I just couldn't cope with the excitement of it all! I stopped enjoying the city and then the opportunity came up to buy the boatyard. Everything came together at the right time. Running the business involves everything from cutting the grass to making sure the boats are safely secured. I take out the rubbish, do the VAT returns and take on the maintenance tasks. It's a glorified caretaker role basically, but it means I can work outside and enjoy the island.

Describe the island.

Ash Island has a weir on either end of it; you can only reach the island by boat or by walking across the lock and weir next door. We've deliberately kept the island fairly wild. This is good for nature and the habitat, plus I like a lot of greenery. Nothing much happens here, which is the way we like it. There are three houses, one of which is mine, and around 50 full-time residential houseboats moored to the island.

We have around 80 residents in total. The atmosphere is very chilled and everyone rubs along fairly well together. Despite the number of people who live here, you don't bump into people a great deal and everyone has their privacy. No one knows who we are or where we are; it's nice to be anonymous.

What kind of people decide to move to the island?

It's a mixture between those who do it for the lifestyle and those who do it because living on a narrowboat is a lot cheaper than living in a flat or house. We also have a steady flow of people who are going through a divorce – it's a cheap, temporary place to stay until the family home is sold.

Describe the Ash Island community.

People who live here because it's cheap only tend to leave when they find partners on the mainland and move in with them. Those who live here for the lifestyle generally stay for years and years. We have everyone from city workers to Tai Chi practitioners. People tend to be a little bit strange to want to live on the river; it's not a normal thing to do. We probably have a more eclectic bunch of people here than you would on the mainland, but it's eclectic in a good way. There used to be much more of a sociable side, but a couple of the more sociable residents died and now it's broken up into lots of smaller groups. We've got a younger, party crowd, older folk, and everyone in between. There are four island babies now, which is the most we've ever had. They range in age from one month to 10 years old. It changes the dynamic and it's nice to hear the laughter of children.

What are the downsides of island life?

It's normally the winters on an island that sort the men from the boys and the women from the girls. You get a few people who buy a houseboat in the summer and sell in the spring because they couldn't bear the winter. There are days when you're coming home from work in the pouring rain, carrying 17 bags of supermarket shopping across the weir. There are days when you just want to use the bathroom as soon as you get home, but you have to empty your chemical toilet before you can do that. There are days when you get home and you're freezing cold, but you've got to light a fire before you can warm up. It's not for everyone. But even if – or when – I win the lottery, I wouldn't live anywhere else.

Do you worry about flooding?

All Thames islands are naturally flat and about 10cm above the river level. When the river was dredged in the 1830s, these dredgings were piled on the flat islands, which is why the centre of the island is a couple of metres higher than the edge. So there's no risk of the water coming up to my house. However, every five years or so we get a lot of rain and the water level comes right up. Then it becomes a little more entertaining getting people on and off the houseboats; some of them only become accessible by a bridge and a step ladder from the island. You worry about peoples' safety a bit more then, particularly if they've had a drink...

You're very close to Taggs Island – how do the islands compare?

Ash Island is the cheaper, wilder island, whereas Taggs Island has manicured lawns; living there is a very different proposition. Taggs Island is mostly characterised by its 'two-storey house boxes'. The local council has said that house boxes are houses that float, whereas houseboats have a pointed front and the ability to propel themselves. This means that new house boxes need planning permission, and since we're in a conservation area, new house boxes won't be allowed on these islands. I'm proud of our eclectic houseboats on Ash Island, and that we'll always mainly have pointy boats here.

What unexpected things have you discovered about Ash Island?

I've done a lot of research into the island. In some history books, there are reports of someone bringing a cow onto the island in the 1890s. It was obviously a big deal back then! Also in the late 19th century, the weather was a lot colder and the river used to freeze over. People used to bring a barbecue onto the ice by the island and serve roast mutton. That happened for a number of years until the ice wasn't thick enough one year, and a whole bunch of people and sheep ended up in the river. We keep our barbecues on dry land nowadays...

ASH ISLAND

Taggs Island

This stretch of the River Thames is known as the Thames Riviera, with some of the UK's most expensive houseboats in the middle of a very sought after area. Like Eel Pie, this is another island with a colourful history of entertainment and dramatic turns of events. The development of the island began in the 1850s, when a local property developer bought the island and evicted squatter families and gypsies living there. Legend has it that a gypsy curse was placed on the island as a result, declaring that people connected with the island would never prosper. The myth was apparently perpetuated when initiatives by different business people always seemed to eventually fail over the decades that followed.

The first business was the Island Hotel – the beer house and skittle alley that moved over from Ash Island – but the business was closed after it failed to flourish. Thomas George Tagg, who the island is still named after today, reopened the property as the Thames Hotel. The next 25 years saw the island do very well as a resort for the wealthy, well-known actors and royalty, including the future King Edward VII. After Thomas Tagg died, a series of events lead to the hotel going bankrupt.

In the early 1900s, Taggs Island was sold to the well-known theatre producer Fred Karno. He opened the Karsino Hotel on the island, complete with continental gardens, sports facilities, a German beer garden and a grand ballroom big enough for 350 people. It was hugely successful for a time, when glamorous and wealthy people from miles around visited regularly. Karno used some of his profits to have a grand houseboat called the Astoria built. It was the most grandiose houseboat of its time and Charlie Chaplin – whom Fred Karno discovered – had his first audition aboard the boat.

Flooding and the impact of World War I took its toll on Karno, and he eventually went bankrupt in the 1920s.

In 1986, Pink Floyd's guitarist David Gilmour bought the Astoria and turned it into a recording studio, after he became tired of recording music in dark, uninspiring studios. Parts of three Pink Floyd albums were recorded on board, as well as Gilmour's solo albums, *On an Island* and *Rattle That Lock*. The Astoria is still moored nearby, in between Taggs Island and Garrick's Ait.

Following the Karno era of Taggs Island, various businessmen came and went. At different points in time, there was a sandy beach, a covered tennis court, a skating rink and an Invacar factory that built three-wheeled cars for disabled drivers. Grand plans for high rise flats, luxurious hotels, restaurants and marinas fell through and the island's dilapidated hotel was scheduled for demolition. Before it was knocked down, scenes from *A Clockwork Orange* were filmed there and a farewell lunch was held in the old grand ballroom, attended by celebrities including Bill Oddie and Eric Idle.

The overgrown island was eventually bought by houseboat owners Gerry and Gillian Braban in 1980. They painstakingly revitalised the island with gardens, palm trees, colourful shrubs, and created a lagoon in the centre of the island for 20 houseboats to moor. Nowadays, there are no houses on the island itself, but the lagoon and outer edge of the island are home to around 60 of the grandest floating houses on the Thames, many of them two-storey. In-keeping with the island's history, residents are musicians, songwriters, TV producers and those working in the creative industries. The island itself is home to spacious gardens and communal areas for the many social events held there, while a road bridge connects islanders to the mainland.

Size and location:
Approximate size: 28,000m²
Coordinates: 51.409, -0.353

Can you visit?
Since the island is owned by residents, only island residents can go there. Get an insight into the island from the Taggs Island website, run by residents: www. taggs-island.com

Carl's tips:
Just across the water from Taggs Island is a café called Thyme by the River – inside the Molesey Boat Club. It's a great spot for tea, cake, lunch or a daytime drink. Sit at one of the tables on the deck outside and you'll have a perfect view of the floating houses of Taggs Island.

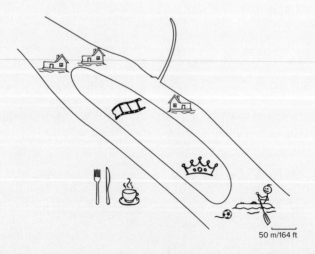

50 m/164 ft

TAGGS ISLAND

Photo: Talented Ladies Club

Suzanne Cave
Actress

Actress and voiceover narrator Suzanne Cave lives on a houseboat on Taggs Island with her husband and children.

Introduce yourself.

I'm an actress, a wife and a mum of two children. I live on Taggs Island in the houseboat I grew up in. My parents are divorced but friendly and both still live on the island. We built my dad an upper storey to his houseboat and we live in the lower storey.

Why did you decide to live on Taggs Island?

I moved here from Liverpool with my family when I was 12. I went away for university and lived in west London after that. My partner is a composer and we wanted to get on the property ladder, but given our professions, we weren't earning much money and couldn't afford to stay in London. Then my dad came up with an idea: we could move into his houseboat and build a second storey for him to live in. It was still cheaper than buying a two bedroom flat in Ealing at the time, so we poured all our money into the project. I've been living on the island again since 2009, although my family's been here for more than 30 years.

Tell us about your work.

My background is in drama, mostly in theatre acting. I've done national tours and worked in London's West End, for plays such as *An Inspector Calls*. Most of my bigger acting jobs were before I had children. I'm still around, but often not as myself, as I now do a lot of voice-over work. I did the *Walking with Cavemen* documentary series for the BBC, I was Angel Destiny for *Captain Scarlet* and I've done a lot for the Discovery Channel. I'm also a trained executive coach and deliver corporate training, fine tuning behaviours in both the public and private sectors.

What is the most unexpected thing that has happened to you on the island?

Four months after moving in, our houseboat sank. It encapsulated everything river dwellers dread. Late one evening, a luxury boat with people drinking and partying went past at a ridiculous speed. A very large wash of water rocked us up and down. Unknown to us at the time, debris from the old Karsino Hotel was underneath our boat and the rocking motion caused us to smash into something sharp, putting a hairline crack in our fibreglass hull. Over two weeks, water gradually seeped in and then we sank very suddenly.

What did you do?

The boat sank right up to the ceiling of the lower storey – the whole place was completely gutted. The amazing thing was the incredible, positive response from the islanders. They helped us salvage whatever we could from the river, they housed us, washed our clothes and put a fund together. Their reaction in such a difficult situation made it a no-brainer to rebuild on the island again. It's such a lovely community.

Are you worried about sinking again?

We've had divers sweep the bottom of the river, so we know there's no debris directly underneath us now. We've got a new steel hull which is stronger than the fibreglass one. We've also got alarm systems in each corner of our hull so if any water ever gets into it we'll know. We probably have the safest boat on the island now!

Describe the Taggs Island community.

For us it's a great balance. We know and have a good relationship with most people on the island, but it doesn't feel like people are in your business. There are lots of friendship groups on the island, but if you want to be private, you can be. We have various social events such as an annual party. Having the water in common makes people amazing at pulling together, especially if there's a crisis. For children growing up on the island, it's like being back in the 1970s. As soon as they're strong enough swimmers, you know they can wander off and be safe.

What's the best thing about living on an island?

Watching the river go by and seeing the effect the different seasons have on the water has a very visceral effect. During summer evenings the island really comes into its own. Most islanders have boats and you'll often see them going out on the water with a glass of wine. The rhythm of life is lovely.

What advice would you give someone hoping to live on a houseboat?

Be prepared to contend with different things than the average person. For example, rowing boats will smash into the side of your houseboat every now and again. Being closer to nature is wonderful, but you have to be prepared to see the cruelty of nature day by day too. It's lovely when you see a duck go past with 11 new ducklings; a few days later there are only six ducklings and you think 'oh crap.'

TAGGS ISLAND

Grant Braban
Owner of Taggs Island

After his parents saved Taggs Island from an uncertain future, Grant took over the reins in the community of 'creatives, dreamers and optimists'.

Tell us about your family's history on Taggs Island.

My mum and dad moved to the island in the summer of 1969 for my dad's work. They rented the smallest houseboat on the island for £6 per week and fell in love with the place. One summer became two summers, which became three summers. A couple of years later, they were a young couple in love, rowing around the island, when they saw a large, unfinished houseboat for sale. It was called KJELL and was built by the daughter of an English industrialist and the owner of Coloroll Wallpaper. She had named the boat after her Swedish boyfriend, who was due to move in with her, but they broke up before this happened. Her family became annoyed at having to store the boat, so they agreed to sell it to my parents for a ridiculously knocked down price of a few thousand pounds. So that got my mum and dad a foothold onto the island and a nice houseboat to go with it. My sister and I came along in the early 1970s and it's been our family home ever since.

How did your parents go from houseboat owners to buying the island?

There were a lot of issues back in those days with rights and who was obliged to provide services to the island's inhabitants. The island was home to a mix of boats with leases and squatters. It was basically derelict, yet the council was obliged to provide access for the residents over the old war-time bridge. The bridge had been assembled temporarily by the Royal Engineers during World War II. It was an important site because Bren guns and bullets were being made on the island. Where most other war-time bridges had been disassembled, the one on Taggs Island had remained for years, and the council eventually closed it down. Everyone on Taggs Island needed the bridge to get to their front doors, so we all campaigned and there were various schemes to try to sort out ownership of the island and the bridge. All

of these fell through, so eventually my mum and dad stepped up to the plate and bought it. They'd arrived on the island skint a few years before and ended up buying an island and a bridge! Not only that, but a condition of the sale was for them to knock the bridge down and build a new one.

How did your parents go about solving the island's problems?

Once they owned the island, it was the hot potato. The council didn't want anything to do with them, yet it was their responsibility to sort out the issue of the bridge and maintain the island for the residents. They had a three year planning battle with the council, who didn't want to approve permission for anything. They tried everything including bungalows, holiday lets, theme park, leisure centre and pet cemetery. All ideas were rejected. They asked the council what they hoped would happen to Taggs Island and were told they hoped the island would sink, along with its residents! We were a shambolic bunch of hippies and dreamers outside of the usually controlled scope of the council. My parents then submitted a plan to add more houseboats to the island by digging a lagoon in the centre. Since the island was already being used for houseboats, they couldn't really say no.

So your parents were the heroes of Taggs Island?

The council thought their plan was going to be an epic failure and put all sorts of conditions on them after granting planning permission. They said we'd look like a swampy caravan park. But it worked. By selling the 20 extra houseboats that fit into the lagoon, they found a way to pay for the bridge. When I think back, it was an incredibly bold manoeuvre by my parents. They were a couple in their 40s with two young kids. They had no experience of high finance, big developments or building bridges. And this was the 1980s, when interest rates for borrowing were above 20%. I can't believe they did it, but thank goodness they did.

Have you always been moored to the same spot?

Before my parents owned the island, we got kicked off our mooring a few times. Our big houseboat would then be towed around to a different spot on the island, which may or may not have been an upgrade. As a kid, it was quite an intriguing experience. I'd just have to pick up my toys from the garden before the boat was disconnected, hop aboard and watch the scenery go by. When we connected back up, we had the same home but a completely different view and garden. It was great – familiar but new.

Describe your childhood on the island.

It was a fantastic place for my sister and I because the whole place was derelict. The Karsino had been knocked down, so there were all sorts of remnants from that. There were abandoned caravans, treehouses and sunken boats. There were about 16 kids on the island and we had free rein. Anyone could go anywhere they wanted, we just had to tell our folks if we were going over the bridge. What freedom! When I was about eight, I remember it occurring to me that I could do whatever I wanted on the island and not get told off, because my dad owned it. One day I came back from school and all the camps, dens and treehouses had been bulldozed because work on the lagoon had started. But even that was fun. Living on an island as a child makes you rubbish at football though. Every time we kicked the ball into the river – which was often – we had to row after it in a boat. Eventually we gave up and just decided to play pirates instead!

What's your role on the island nowadays?

I'm in charge of the family business as the principal freeholder. In essence, I manage the island. The residents used to manage it, but it didn't really work, so now my job is a benign dictator. Instead of running it by committee, I just say what gets done! It works much better that way. Before that, I spent a number of years flying helicopters in Australia. I came back – initially for a month in between contracts – but I fell in love with the island again and took on the family business.

What kind of people does the island attract?

I'd describe them as dreamers, creatives and optimists, on the whole. Not everyone's very nautical, despite the fact we all live on houseboats. We're all hippies at heart – although some bury their inner hippy a bit deeper than others. Once people move here, they gradually bring their circle of travel closer and closer to the island, until they eventually try to stay on the island as much as possible. People who used to commute up to London find jobs closer by or work from home. For example, one of our residents used to be a customs agent at the airport and now I employ him as a sewage engineer and gardener on the island.

How do people describe their experiences of Taggs Island?

Everyone always says that as soon as they get to the top of the bridge on their way home, they suddenly feel a lot calmer. They all say that unprompted, so it must be some kind of phenomenon. I feel it myself. People get the same effect when they go out on their boat on the river. After a stressful day, you only have to travel 100 metres up the river to feel an amazing calmness. It's a slow pace of life and everyone waves to each other. It's idyllic.

Would you ever leave the island?

I think I'm here to stay. Having moved back from Australia, it feels like home. My mates joke that I get a nosebleed every time I cross the bridge!

Have you had any bizarre experiences on the island?

We have filming on the island sometimes, which makes it look completely different. Recently Disney came along to film for a couple of days and every tree was filled with fairy lights. I also had a German TV crew follow me around one day, for a programme about people who live and work on the London waterways. They spent the whole day laughing! They followed me in my joke pirate paddle steamer boat to Thyme by the River, the local café at the rowing club, where I ate breakfast and checked my emails. They filmed me wandering around the island, handing our random bits of paper to residents. Then they set up a scene where I was telling off teenagers messing around on the bridge, while I was on my joke paddle steamer, with a glass of wine in my hand!

TAGGS ISLAND

Astoria story

Words: Langley Iddins

Graphic artist Langley Iddins is the caretaker of the Astoria houseboat. Formerly built by Fred Karno, it's now owned by Pink Floyd's David Gilmour. Surrounded by the islands so important in its history, the Astoria continues to be an icon of this stretch of the River Thames to this day.

Astoria is grand. The interior of the boat is high Edwardian ornate splendour, like a vast first-class suite lifted off RMS Titanic. She was built in 1911 for the impresario Fred Karno. The designer was Billy Day, master carpenter at Karno's 'Fun Factory'. Karno demanded that she be the best houseboat on the Thames.

My first visit was in March 1985, when she was still owned by the Daly family. Ed Daly, an American businessman and the owner of World Airways, was known among many other things for his humanitarian efforts during the Vietnam War. He had bought the Astoria in 1971 and after he died in 1984, his first wife Joan Daly inherited his property and fortune.

Mrs Daly put the Astoria up for sale in 1985. She was bought by a friend of mine, Colin Hunter. Colin's intention was to sell the boat and keep the land to satisfy his wife's passion for gardening. Meanwhile he invited me to live on the boat and take care of her.

A year after I came to live here, she was sold to David Gilmour, who very kindly let me stay on in return for taking care of the place and looking after the garden. David, who at the time lived three miles upstream in Sunbury-on-Thames, installed a recording studio on the boat. The dining room became a 'live room', the saloon became a 'control room' and the main bedroom a 'machine room'. The rest of the boat remained more or less as she had been since 1911.

Over the years the recording studio has been used by David and his bandmates. Occasionally, he has loaned the studio to musician friends too. These days the studio is rarely used for recording. It is, however, used by David and his sound engineers for mixing. The boat provides the perfect environment for the intense concentration this particular task requires.

Everyone who comes here falls in love with the place. It's a perfect marriage of boat, garden and river. There are many magical features. The 700 panes of bevelled glass set in gun metal window frames create dancing lights on the walls and ceilings when the sun is reflected off the surface of the river. The timbers from the wooden hull below the oak floors emit a comforting smell. The mahogany doors and panelling exude a heady mix of polish and varnish. And the upper deck is basically an incredible 150 m² dance floor.

The garden of the Astoria was part of the riverside estate of the actor and playwright David Garrick. The magic both he and the artist Johan Zoffany – who painted many scenes of the garden – discovered here in the mid-18th century remains. I'm sure that people who come and make music here pick up on this.

It's an earthly and watery idyll. I am surely one of the world's luckiest.

Duck Eyot

This tiny island has just a few weeping willow trees and, true to its name, a whole lot of ducks.

Size and location
Approximate size: 280m²
Coordinates: 51.4103, -0.3556

Can you visit?
Yes, accessible by boat only.

Carl's tips:
Catch a glimpse of Duck Eyot by walking along the Thames Path on the Molesey side of the river.

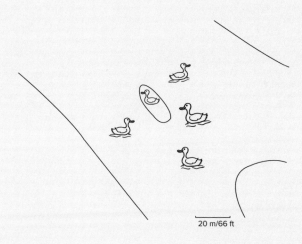

20 m/66 ft

Garrick's Ait

This island is only accessible by boat and has 26 houses. Garrick's Ait is named after actor David Garrick, whose villa and Grade 1 listed *Temple to Shakespeare* – reportedly the world's only shrine to Shakespeare – are on the riverbank. He used the island to entertain guests. The island was clearly used for a long time before Garrick, as a flint axe has been found on the island, thought to date back to at least 4000BC. The island was a popular place for camping and picnics during the early 1900s, which were gradually replaced by wooden summer cabins and eventually houses. Nowadays, islanders live on relatively small plots and use rowing boats or motorised boats to get over to the mainland when they need to. On the Molesey bank, the park is the site of the former Hurst Park Racecourse, which operated from 1890 until the 1960s.

Size and location:
Approximate size: 5,500m²
Coordinates: 51.4116, -0.3604

Can you visit?
No, accessible to homeowners only.

Carl's tips:
Garrick's Ait is a lot closer to the Molesey side of the riverbank than the Hampton side, so walking along the Thames Path is the perfect way to have a look at the island.

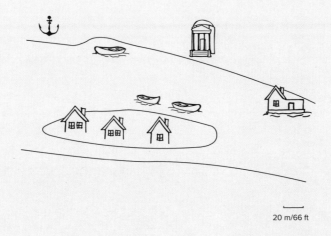

20 m/66 ft

GARRICK'S AIT

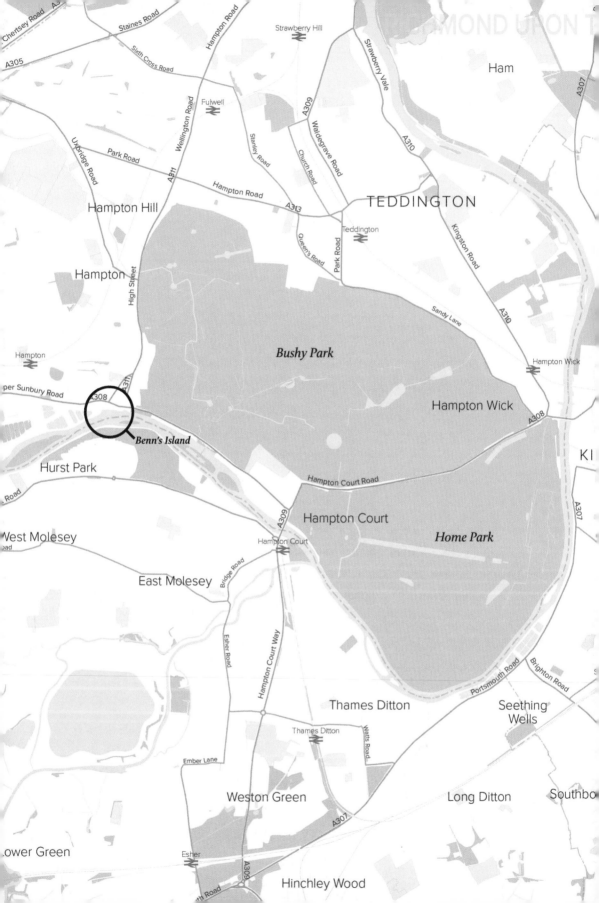

Benn's Island

This small island is home to the Hampton Sailing Club and there's only enough space on the island for the club house and a few boats. Going right past the island is a chain link ferry that connects the two riverbanks.

Size and location:
Approximate size: 1,000m²
Coordinates: 51.412, -0.363

Can you visit?
No, accessible to members of the sailing club only. Look out for occasional events and family fun days: www.hamptonsailingclub.com

Carl's tips:
Get on the chain link ferry, which operates seasonally, for the perfect way to catch a glimpse of the island. Hampton Ferry Boathouse (Thames Street, TW12 2EW, www. hamptonferryboathouse.co.uk) also has boats available to hire, ideal for exploring the many fascinating islands on this stretch of the river.

20 m/66 ft

Peter Norrey
Film editor

*BAFTA award winning Peter discovered creative inspiration along with a millionaire's view
when he moved to Garrick's Ait, where he lives with his wife and son.*

Introduce yourself.

I was an art student who moved from north Wales to Plymouth to be a photographer, but came out the other side as a film editor. I'm still not quite sure how that happened! I gained work experience as an assistant on films like *The Borrowers* before moving into food and lifestyle programmes for chefs including Rick Stein and Keith Floyd. I wanted to feel the race of London living – and the film industry elsewhere in the UK is limited – so I moved to London to work in television, which I did for a number of years. I gradually moved into longer form work – such as feature documentaries and films – which is what I do now. I've done some directing and I like doing it, but I'm leagues ahead in my film editing because I didn't really focus on developing my directing career. But I direct the occasional film because as a film editor, you have to understand the directing side, and it's only by doing it that you get a very good understanding of it.

What have been the highlights of your career?

It takes years of experience to hone the skill, which I only value now in hindsight. After 20 years of practice I understand the language, craft, workflow and the way things need to be in a film. I won a BAFTA for editing the film *SAS Embassy Siege* in 2003 and I've had a couple of nominations since then. I recently did a feature film for cinema release with Damien Hirst about the story of ancient art treasures found under the ocean. That was really exciting and I think I'd like to do more long form cinema projects like that. It allows you to find some form of perfection, or at least try to attain something that's the very best you can do.

What were you looking for in a home before you arrived on Garrick's Ait?

My wife Cora and I were like a lot of couples living in rented accommodation in south London. We were living around bankers and hedge fund managers, who all had the same window shutters and BMWs parked outside. It wasn't a creative community at all and not somewhere we wanted to live permanently. We were looking at what we could do with the money we had, which wasn't an enormous amount, so we had to be quite ingenious with what we did have. We started looking on the outskirts of London and liked the Hampton area – it felt like a village and was different and interesting.

Tell us your story of discovering the island.

When I saw the house on Garrick's Ait advertised, I didn't realise it was on an island! The estate agent confirmed the appointment and said she'd meet us on the boat – I wondered what she was talking about. We were sceptical but decided to go anyway. The day we visited was beautiful. It was warm, the water was still and the doors were wide open in the house. Cora's eyes lit up. The view from the deck was a millionaire's view. I imagined waking up to that every day – it really is something to look at, rather than a grey road. The house itself is open plan, which also appealed, because we're not very tidy! We decided to go for it. We put all our savings in and managed to get a mortgage. We did it on a whim, quite prepared to pack it all up if it wasn't right. We've been here since 2013 and now the thought of living anywhere else is really unappealing.

What were the early days like?

We spent the first year bumping into the quay, bouncing around the river and being rescued by other islanders! Now we've got hold of it – we understand boats, the terminology and the engines. Three months after we moved in was the notorious 2013 Thames flood. It rained and rained. The water came within half a metre of the house – it was scary and we felt at risk. The water was apparently flowing at 400 tonnes per second. It was unsafe to go across in the boat, so we got a lift off the island and stayed with friends for a week. We thought we'd been sold a dead duck, assuming this happened every year. After speaking to other islanders, some of whose properties had been in their families for generations, they said it was unprecedented. Every year since, it's been absolutely fine. In fact, the island is higher than the London floodplain, so if Garrick's Ait flooded, places like Wandsworth and Chiswick in London would also be in serious trouble.

Did anything else come as a surprise?

It's more of an active lifestyle than I imagined. You're always doing something: tugging boats, tying off boats and taking your bins across the river. I realised how life before was quite sedentary in comparison. You also have to learn new things quickly. I was away filming in the middle of winter once and the lights stopped working on our boat. Cora downloaded a YouTube video and worked out 12V electrical systems so she could fix it! There's a practical edge to life, which we find quite appealing.

What feeling does living on an island give you?

When you leave to go to work in the morning, it's an event to leave the island behind. It feels cosy, intimate, quiet and small. It's not brash or brazen in any way. I row across, which takes just two or three minutes and it gives you a taste of the day. Sometimes that row is blowy, wet and horrible. Other times it's just so beautiful, moonlit and calm. Whatever the weather is, you feel it and you're in it. That was part of the appeal of living on the island. You're living in nature more than you would do on a street. Crossing the river gives a nice divide in life too – when you come home, you leave everything behind on the other side.

Describe the Garrick's Ait community.

I think people who live on an island want to escape something of the world. Not everything, but something. As a result, everyone is quite re-spectful of each other's space, peace and quiet. There seems to be an etiquette that people keep themselves to themselves. We don't just turn up at people's houses; we call ahead, even if it's just two doors down. I'd describe the community as beautifully dysfunctional! People have an idealised version of what community life is, but you have to work hard to make a community work. It takes effort to get organised and work together, but it's sometimes difficult because we're an island of individuals. There's also an unspoken rule that if you have a problem, you can call a neighbour, any time of the day or night. Things do happen. We've run out of petrol and drifted down the river late at night. Neighbours help out without question, a lot more than I've experienced anywhere else.

Would you ever leave the island?

We have a son now and so far we've made it work, but we know the house might not be big enough forever. But we're always trying to figure out how to make it work for as long as possible.

Does the island inspire creativity?

Creativity is a nurtured commodity. You've got to develop it and you need inspiration. For me, that's light, changing seasons, space, water and things going on. I get a feeling of escape on the island and that leads to being able to focus on my work and creativity.

How do people react when you tell them you live on an island?

Telling new people where we live is always fascinating. They ask if we have things like toilets and electricity – some of the questions are amazing! I love the look on friends' faces when we bring them across. We have dinner or a barbecue on the terrace and they fall in love with it as well.

TEMPLE TO SHAKESPEARE - PHOTO: PETER NORREY

Laurie Gibbs
Conservator

Originally from France, conservator Laurie works at Hampton Court Palace. She moved to Garrick's Ait for a better commute to work and discovered a whole new way of life

How did you discover Garrick's Ait?

I have worked as a conservator at Hampton Court Palace since the late 1990s. For 17 of those years I had a long, painful commute from Crystal Palace, which I became thoroughly fed up with. My husband's a food specialist and when he got a job in Richmond, we decided it was time to move. Our only criteria were that we wanted somewhere bright, quiet and within walking or cycling distance of Hampton Court Palace. We saw a house for sale on Garrick's Ait and went to visit. It was so completely different to anything else we'd seen and it answered all our criteria. We face the park, so the only noise we get is from ducks, geese and barking dogs. It's nice and bright, and I can walk to work in 20 minutes from the riverbank.

Tell us about working at Hampton Court Palace.

I used to work in the catering trade and re-trained in my mid-30s. I went to City and Guilds of London art school and did a degree in conservation. When I was a student, I worked for Hampton Court Palace, so it was natural that I should apply for whatever jobs they had available. I work as a preventive conservator, which is all about looking after interiors and objects in museums or historic houses. I make sure objects don't deteriorate through too much light, heat or fluctuation in humidity. At Hampton Court Palace, there's a much larger remit than most preventive conservators have, as we look after the building wholesale. A lot of functions, events and filming happen at the palace, so I help to ensure they go smoothly without causing any damage. It's a fascinating job.

Describe the experience of moving onto the island.

We moved in 2014 – the year of all the flooding – which meant we exchanged contracts in January but couldn't move in for another 10 weeks because the whole local area was flooded. The lorry with our furniture on wouldn't have been able to reach the riverbank, and the Environment Agency had a red flag on the river, meaning you're not supposed to use it. It was really miserable for us – we used to go and stand in front of our house on the river's edge, looking at the turmoil of the water. Our house was absolutely fine because it's high enough, but we wondered when on earth we were going to be able to move in. Nevertheless, we never had any doubt about the fact that we'd made the right decision.

How did your friends react when you told them you were going to live on an island?

There was no halfway house. People were either really envious or thought we were absolutely crazy!

What is island living like?

Island living is out of peoples' comfort zones, but when you look at the minutiae of going back and forth – which is about a three-minute boat ride – it's really not much hard work. It's just something else to get used to. I live in a normal house that has gas, electricity and broadband, plus I can flush my toilet! It's not like living in a boat or a caravan. Our houses are quite close together, so it's more akin to a terraced house, although we are detached. The only different thing we have to do is take our dustbins across the river to some very large bins in the park.

Is there a community spirit?

We very quickly realised there's a real community spirit because we have to depend on each other. As soon as we moved in, we were given a list of all the islanders' email addresses and phone numbers. For six months of the year there's a local ferry that we can ask to drop us home if we're desperate. But for the other six months of the year we're on our own, so we rely on each other. If anybody has engine problems, we knock on each other's doors and ask for a lift. It forces us into being quite a close community, which is really nice.

What are the other islanders like?

There were previously several actors and actresses on the island. Like a lot of the River Thames islands, it had a very bohemian feel to it, which attracted a lot of people from creative industries. Now there's an extremely varied slice of society. We have a few retired people, the person who runs the ferry, a lecturer in neuroscience, a web designer, a graphic designer, people who work in retail, two retired head teachers, a civil servant and a dog groomer. Our youngest member is six months old and the oldest is in his mid-70s.

What's the best thing about living on the island?

We don't get door-to-door salesmen and it's a pretty safe environment. My nephew came to stay with me recently and I got a call from one of my neighbours telling me there was someone they didn't recognise on my deck. So you have to tell your neighbours when you have visitors! If you're a cat lover like me, it's also very safe for cats; there's no risk of them getting run over here. We have great community rituals as an island too. Sometimes we'll take a few boats to go to the pub together or for an annual Christmas shopping and lunch trip to Kingston.

What's the most inconvenient thing about living on an island?

Since Garrick's Ait doesn't have a bridge, everything you need to do requires a boat. When I first arrived here, I drew up a list of everything I hated about boats. It's very difficult to do anything in heels. Boats are always wet at the bottom and it doesn't help that we live in a country where it rains. The Thames is either brown or green or colour, so you spend your life cleaning. Boats are slightly banana shaped too, yet you always moor onto something straight. And finally, you always have to climb up to get out of a boat – everyone on the island has one of those little steps kids use to clean their teeth because they need it to get out of their boats.

Did you find a solution to your boat woes?

We saved for almost four years to have a boat built to our specification. It's got a flat base that you can stand on – so it doesn't fill up when it rains. It's got a covering so there's shelter in the rain too. And it's level with our mooring, so we can literally just step on and off. It's not a conventional boat – some would call it quirky – but we had it built to future-proof us so we can stay on the island as we get older. People tend to stop living on the island when they can no longer get in and out of their boats.

Have your hobbies changed since moving to the island?

Definitely! Some nights I pick my husband up in the boat and we spontaneously decide to do a trip around one of the nearby islands. As long as it's not raining, it's a really pleasant thing to do. If we go around sunset, the geese fly in formation above our heads. We're a lot closer to nature in general now. Two swans nested on some empty land next to us once, but it was too tall and after they left for a short while, they couldn't get back on-land to take care of their cygnets. We had to scoop them out and take care of them until they were big enough to leave. They come by to visit every now and again – we know they're our boys because they hop onto the deck, have a look at where their nest was and then leave again.

What feeling do you get when you return home to Garrick's Ait?

Even if we've been on holiday somewhere nice, we arrive at the riverside, look at the Thames and feel immediately at home. Our boat will be waiting for us – because one of our neighbours will have cared enough to drop it off for us – and then we travel across to the island. We immediately feel we have some space away from the rest of the crazy world.

What's the funniest thing about living on the island?

People don't realise how well sound carries over the water. Sometimes passers-by stand on the riverbank and talk about us or our house, not realising we can hear them perfectly! Another funny thing is that people always wave to you when they're in a boat and you're expected to wave back. It's odd when you think about it, because on land you don't wave to people from your car. The river is really busy during the summertime and we regularly see boating stag parties too; for some reason they're always wearing sombreros. We look forward to a break from waving in the winter!

GARRICK'S AIT

Jonathan Steel
Retired designer

*Keen rower Jonathan Steel bought a plot on Garrick's Ait after
witnessing a fire on the island.*

How did you first discover Garrick's Ait?

I've been a passionate rower for almost my whole life. In 1970, I moved to Molesey Boat Club from Putney and subsequently rowed past Garrick's Ait many times. One day I was rowing past as a huge fire had taken hold on the island. I was 30 metres away but I could still feel the heat on my face – it was very frightening. A while later, I put a bid in for the plot and got it. I bought a house to my specification from Finland, which is very eco-friendly and warm in the winter. I've lived here since the early 2000s.

What are your favourite things about your spot of the River Thames?

I love the tradition of the river, both the working Thames as well as the recreational Thames. There's some fascinating history in this area, from the Molesey Regatta which would have finished right opposite my house, to Fred Karno's old Astoria houseboat. Karno was like the Donald Trump of the 1890s – he had this huge houseboat built so it would fit a 100-piece orchestra on its roof. The story is that he never took his wife to see the boat, just his mistresses. Now it's David Gilmour's houseboat. I was lucky enough to have a tour of it and it's incredible.

How did you wangle a tour of the Astoria?

I know the caretaker, who is also a really good designer and calligrapher. He indulged me with an inspection. When you build something on a boat, it's all about size and how you can fit everything in. It's even got a marble bathroom in it.

Tell us about the Garrick's Ait community.

When we mix there's usually an awful lot of wine involved! We tend to do our own thing most of the time. I think this has a lot to do with the fact all our houses face outwards, so we live our lives from the front of the house rather than the back. There's definitely an island spirit though and we help each other out a lot.

What advice would you give someone hoping to live on a River Thames island?

Prepare for a slightly different way of life. It's not eccentric, but it isn't the norm. You need to have a bit of self-sufficiency. And you need a good memory. You don't want to jump in the boat to the mainland to get some vegetables, only to forget what you went out for!

What are the practical issues of living on an island?

I'm quite defensive about this. Many people living in the London outskirts can't park their car outside their house. All we've got to do is row across in a boat. It's absolutely fine for almost all the year, except when the stream occasionally runs very fast and we have to be a bit more careful. All you need is a nice big American fridge and a rack full of wine to keep you tided over!

Platt's Eyot

This island surrounded by boats of various shapes and sizes is connected to the mainland by a pedestrian suspension bridge that was built in 1941. It's an island of two halves, with a bustling array of light industry happening at one end and an overgrown wilderness at the other, which is an important spot for nature conservation. One of the river's tallest islands, dumped earth from the excavations of nearby reservoirs is partly responsible for the steep banks.

The island's history is mostly in boat building and in the late 1800s, the island was also known for recharging the batteries of electric canoes, popular on the river at the time. Thorneycroft boat builders later took over the business, whose boats with Rolls Royce engines took many world speed records. Around this time, Thomas Tagg built a boatyard and house on the island before he moved to the now-called Taggs Island.

The most notable time in the island's history starts during World War I, when the Royal Navy's CMB (coastal motor boat) torpedoes were built in secret inside four huge boat sheds. These camouflaged boat sheds were constructed using a rare design technique and they are now listed buildings, regularly inspected by the Historic England organisation. The first ever aircraft carrier is also thought to have been built on Platt's Eyot, while small naval craft were built there throughout both world wars.

Nowadays, the area of boatsheds on the island have Grade II listed status and the old Tagg house is being used as offices. There have been many bids by developers to build on the island over the decades, but marrying conservation with development has proved difficult in terms of gaining permission. Those living and working on the island are a creative bunch and include graphic designers, furniture makers, beer brewers and music producers. Musicians ranging from Eric Clapton to the Spice Girls have recorded on the island.

Size and location
Approximate size: 42,500m²
Coordinates: 51.410, -0.372

Can you visit?
It's a private island, so only residents, business owners or visitors to the businesses are allowed on the island.

Carl's tips:
The best views of the island are from the Platt's Eyot car park on the Hampton side of the river, or from the Thames Path surrounded by parkland on the other side.

Steve Lyon
Music producer

With a studio located on Platt's Eyot, Steve is one of a thriving community of creatives and entrepreneurs on the island. Known for working with the likes of Depeche Mode and The Cure, the most famous visitor to his island studio was Eric Clapton.

Introduce yourself.

I'm a music producer, engineer and mixer; I started out at Air Studios in central London. I've worked with a huge range of musicians and bands including Paul McCartney, Depeche Mode and The Cure. Now I work with a few American bands and some Italian artists. I spend my time working at my studio on Platt's Eyot and travelling around the world for work.

How did you discover Platt's Eyot?

I was looking for a space where I could set up my own gear to record an album with Suzerain, a band I've been working with for several years now. The guitarist asked if I'd heard of Platt's Eyot. Although I lived just down the road in Twickenham, I'd never heard of it. We jumped in the car, parked up and walked over the bridge. I thought it was great, so I got in touch with the management agency to see if they had any space available.

Tell us about your studio.

When I first saw the space inside a former industrial building, I could see that someone had already tried to convert it into a recording studio or a radio station. I'm not quite sure what they were doing, but they'd divided up some of the space and built a room inside a room. It was covered in dust when I first arrived and pigeons and mice had been in there. It wasn't very pleasant, but the space itself was amazing. I only wanted it for a few months to record the album with the band, but it was only available for a longer let. After much deliberation, I decided to take it on full time. It was never my intention to have my own studio, but now I'm very glad I do. It's invaluable to me. It's also a space that people find inspiring and adaptable for photo and video shoots, so a lot of artists come in for that too.

Who's the most well-known visitor to your studio?

Eric Clapton came in a few years ago. I used to work for Glyn Johns, who worked with everyone from Led Zeppelin to The Rolling Stones. He was also Eric's producer for a while in the 1970s. Off the back of that, Eric's manager phoned me and said: 'Mr Clapton would like to come in.' It wasn't a phone call I was expecting! They wanted me to work with them on a project together with Chris Barber, the famous jazz musician and trombonist. I was doing some building work to the studio at the time, so when Eric walked through the door, there were bags of sand on the floor and a hole in the wall! It didn't seem to faze him at all. He spent a couple of days on the island and it was great.

Describe the feeling on Platt's Eyot.

I fell in love with the island very quickly. It's got a lot of character and the people are really nice – we all look out for each other. People who come over to work with me love it too. Even in the middle of winter or if it's pouring down with rain, the atmosphere is still fantastic. You can sit outside on a bench and there's no-one around – you don't feel like you're in London at all. There's also a really cool old wooden shack at the upriver end of the island. It's too dilapidated to get close to now, but it's all very beaten up and characterful. There's a lot to discover on the island. I have people coming and going from my studio all the time. I can leave the door open and enjoy the environment, which includes the occasional duck walking in and out!

Why do you think the River Thames islands have attracted people from the music industry?

The islands have always been a little bit of a bohemian sanctuary away from the mainland. My mum and her mates used to go to the club on Eel Pie Island in the 1960s, Pete Townsend has his Eel Pie Studios nearby and David Gilmour from Pink Floyd has his houseboat on the river near Hampton Court. There's also a barge on Ash Island that can be rented out via Airbnb; I've organised for bands to stay there before and they absolutely love it. The area has always been quite seductive for musicians. Music also brings noise with it, and some people don't like that. Finding somewhere you don't have to worry about that is a godsend.

What are your hopes for the island in the future?

I'd like to be able to do a bit more maintenance and upkeep on the outside of my building. I'm restricted in this respect because it's classified as a historic building. As a result, some buildings and shipyards on the island are becoming dilapidated. The historic nature of the island also means it's difficult for developers to get planning permission. I think they'd like to turn the island into residential buildings and make loads of money, which would be great for them but a terrible shame for the island. It's nice to have a little bohemian society in the middle of the River Thames. Long may it stay that way.

What's the most interesting thing you've discovered on the island?

A lovely old gentleman randomly knocked on my door a few years ago and told me there was a bomb shelter underneath my building. He knew the island from years ago. There's no obvious sign of the bomb shelter being there, but since Platt's Eyot was important during both World Wars, it wouldn't surprise me if there is one.

What's the most unexpected thing that has happened to you on the island?

It's the fantastic mixture of work happening on the island that brings unexpected situations. We've got everything from a prosthetic limb company to craft beer brewers. There used to be a crab factory next to me called Seafood & Eat It. They've moved to Swan Island in Twickenham now, but I used to enjoy a chat with them when we bumped into each other. On occasion, I'd come back to the studio and there would be a little bag of crab meat by my door. That's a bit of a random offering to return to!

Find out more about Steve Lyon at www.steve-lyon.com and www.panicbuttonstudios.com

PLATT'S EYOT

Photo: Martin James Lewis

Brian Watson

Brewer

Beer entrepreneur Brian had a career in television before setting up ODDLY Beer on Platt's Eyot.

Tell us about your background.

I worked in television for 26 years before setting up my own brewery. I started out in editing, but my qualifications are in IT, so I ended up as the CIO for a global media company. I had the idea of setting up a brewery while I was in that job, but I didn't do anything about it. Then I was made redundant and decided I didn't want another office job. I started working in some of the smaller London breweries – as many as would have me. I had no commercial experience of brewing at all, so I learned loads. But what I got really switched onto was the community of London brewers – they're a great bunch doing business in a lovely way. I wanted to be a part of it.

How did you first set up?

I built a cabin in my back garden, got it licensed and built a brewery in it. Pretty much straight away I realised it was too small – and certainly too small for a commercial venture. So I called in some favours, borrowed some larger brewery kit and started making beer commercially. I love making beer, and I think you can taste whether someone cares about what they're producing. And I really do care about what I'm doing – it matters a lot to me. I brew beers that interest me and are interesting to make, and I hope they fire the imagination in other people. I vacillate between making traditional beers and weird and wacky ones – it pushes my abilities.

How did you discover Platt's Eyot?

I was looking for a place to build my own brewery, but everything was so expensive. One day, I received a property alert about a space on an island. The rent was good, but I thought it would be too impractical for my business. My partner was intrigued and said we should go and have a look anyway – she loves property, especially if she can have a good poke around! So we arrived on Platt's Eyot and I immediately listed the many reasons why we shouldn't take the space: there was no plumbing, no electricity, no heating and the building was derelict. And, as if that wasn't enough, access is by a narrow footbridge, so getting anything on and off would be a nightmare. But, despite everything, we loved the island – it's a strange, other-worldly place – so we decided to take on the building and I immediately set about cleaning and repairing it, so I could install a brewery.

What is the most impractical thing about being located on an island?

Dealing with bottle deliveries is particularly trying! Any other brewery, on receiving a few palettes of bottles, would have them safely wheeled inside the warehouse in a matter of minutes. For me, it takes two people 10 hours to move three palettes of bottles from the car park on the riverbank to my unit on the island, because it all has to be done manually over the footbridge. Having bottles delivered was my go-to reason for not moving onto the island, because they are the most difficult thing to lift. But now, I'd be very sorry to leave Platt's Eyot. As we grow, there are tools and devices I could invest in to make my life easier. A boat, for example!

Does anything else make life difficult?

The winters are freezing – really bitter! From January to March last winter, I spent eight hours a day shivering next to the wood-burning stove – and I don't feel the cold much. The roof leaked so much when I first moved in that when it rained, it rained indoors! But that's been repaired now. Despite the difficulties, I still get a buzz every time I walk in. Partly because I've got my own brewery, which is exciting, but also because of the island and its community.

How has your day-to-day working life changed now you have a brewery on an island?

I now have a sense of being close to nature. I'm doing something quite industrial in a big shed, but I'm on the riverbank surrounded by ducks, swans, all kinds of other birds, insects, fish and so many overgrown and wild plants, including hops. It's an interesting juxtaposition. I love to stand and stare at the river, watching the wildlife and boats go past. It's quite beautiful. You can't say that about an office job.

What do you do when you're not brewing on Platt's Eyot?

My business plan – scrawled on a sheet of paper – says I should be out selling my beer. But I'm the worst salesperson in the country! I spent most of my career being sold to; it's a process I don't enjoy, so I'm not very good at selling. I'm much better at talking to drinkers, so I go to a lot of festivals and sell directly to the public. I always come away with a sore throat because we natter for hours. It's good fun and I get lots of positive feedback, so it's energising for me to do that sort of thing.

We're thirsty – where else can we find your beer?

I really like the micro-pubs in Thanet, Kent – and not just because some of them stock my beer! They're a return to what pubs used to be, which is about local communities coming together and knowing each other. Some can only fit 10 or 20 people inside, but they always have interesting beers to try. They make a living, but they'll never make a fortune. They keep their prices low for their customers, so I try to sell to them at a favourable price they can afford. I'm discovering micro-pubs in London, too, such as The Dodo in Hanwell, and a few have taken my beer. I've also collaborated with two other small breweries in north London, The Muswell Hillbilly Brewers and Earth Ales, to

open a bottle shop called Bottle Shop Heroes in Wood Green.

Describe the feeling on Platt's Eyot.

Platt's Eyot has a fascinating boat building history, which dates back to the 1860s. Some of the buildings are First World War boat sheds, but everything is pretty run down now. There's such a range of creative businesses, from a design agency to recording studios. And, of course, there are still boat builders. There's also a guy who makes prosthetic limbs, who uses part of an arm to wedge open his door. It's quite alarming the first time you see it! When you walk across the bridge onto the island, you immediately sense a different atmosphere. You feel as though you're in another world. I was talking to a guy who's been on the island for 25 years and he says he still gets that special feeling when he walks across the bridge. Everyone I've brought to the island just loves it – even people who I thought might not get it.

What do you hope for the island in the future?

Developers have wanted to build luxury houses on the island for years, which would involve demolishing most of the old sheds and other buildings, and stripping back the trees and plants. Some people might look at how dilapidated everything is and think that would be a good idea, but there's so much character, history and value in what's here, it would be a shame. I would rather see the existing buildings better maintained. If there has to be some redevelopment, then I think there's great potential to make it an alternative commercial and entertainment spot, with cafés and maybe even a bar!

How does the island inspire you creatively?

Since moving to the island, I've got into foraging and some of the ingredients I've gathered have inspired new beers – blackberries, rose-hips and wild hops, for example. I have recently collaborated with a brewer friend and we have made a Champagne-style beer with elderflower collected from the island. There's a lot of wild rocket growing, too – I haven't thought what to do with that yet!

Find out more about ODDLY Beer:
www.oddlybeer.com

PLATT'S EYOT

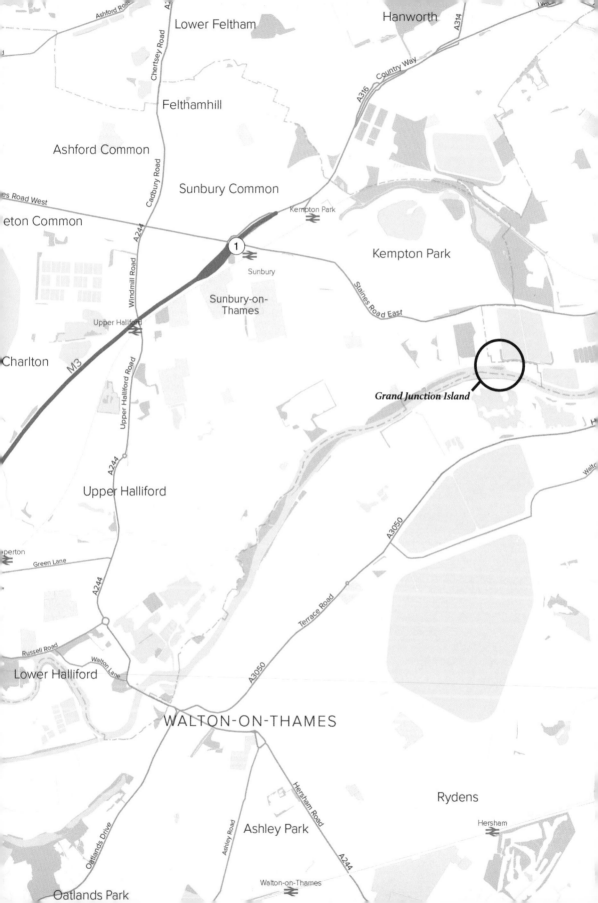

Grand Junction Island

Connected to the riverbank by a footbridge, the island is accessed by a gate to which only homeowners have a key. There are no permanent dwellings on the island itself, just a collection of six weekend chalets with moorings. Londoners used to come down to islands on the River Thames for weekends away and this is one of the few islands on the river where this still happens.

Size and location
Approximate size: 2,500m²
Coordinates: 51.410, -0.389

Can you visit?
No, only homeowners can access the island.

Carl's tips:
You can just about catch a glimpse of the island from the Thames Path on the Molesey side of the river, although the path can be fairly thickly wooded at certain times of the year.

20 m/66 ft

Sunbury Court Island

This island is home to 29 densely developed timber-framed houses and bungalows accessed from a central pathway. Many of the houses have moorings on both sides. It's connected to the mainland by a pedestrian bridge. The local area is home to many film studios, so a number of the former residents were actors, including Hollywood actors Ben Lyon, Bebe Daniels and *Coronation Street* actor Pat Phoenix and her husband Anthony Booth, the father of Cherie Blair.

Size and location
Approximate size: 12,500m²
Coordinates: 51.409, -0.395

Can you visit?
No, only homeowners can access the island,

Carl's tips:
The best spot to get a look of the island is from the Thames Path on the Molesey side of the river. If you want to get a taste of island living for yourself, bed and breakfast accommodation is available at Hunter's Lodge (www.bedandbreakfasts.co.uk).

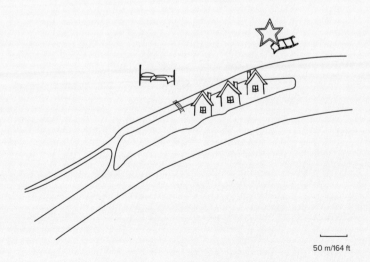

50 m/164 ft

Rivermead Island

A privately owned, publicly accessible, uninhabited island, Rivermead Island is reached by an arched footbridge. It used to be known for its large open-air swimming pool, which was closed and filled in in 1980. Nowadays, it is open parkland with some wooded areas and some sandy beaches. It occasionally floods and was completely submerged during the floods of February 2014. The island is best known for the annual Sunbury Amateur Regatta (www.sunburyregatta.com), which has been happening every August since the late 19th century. There are boating activities, stalls with food, music and fireworks. The rest of the year it's ideal for quiet walks and picnics.

Size and location:
Approximate size: 31,500m²
Coordinates: 51.407, -0.401

Can you visit?
Yes, cross via the footbridge.

Carl's tips:
Go for a wander around the island any time of year. A short walk away is the 18th century Sunbury Walled Garden (Pantiles Court, Thames Street, TW16 6AB) and The Sunbury Embroidery Gallery, ideal for a tea and cake stop.

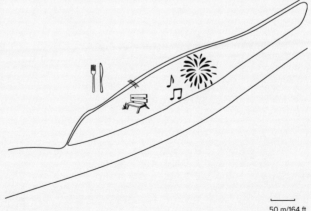

50 m/164 ft

Sunbury Lock Ait

An uninhabited lock island, Sunbury Lock Ait is accessible by footbridge and is connected by a large weir to Wheatley's Eyot next door. There's a long history of human settlement on the island, with human remains found from as long ago as 10,000BC. Tradesmen used to meet for raucous get-togethers in the early 1900s, until Sunbury villagers complained about the noise. The island was home to gun emplacements during World War II to help protect the lock and reservoirs in the local area. Nowadays the island is home to the Middle Thames Yacht Club and public land with a slightly overgrown, wild feeling.

Size and location:
Approximate size: 30,000m²
Coordinates: 51.404, -0.410

Can you visit?
Yes, cross via the footbridge.

Carl's tips:
Take in this lock island by walking along the Thames Path on the Walton-on-Thames riverbank. You can spot the tip of the island from The Weir Hotel (Waterside Drive, KT12 2JB) and pub – which has a lot of outdoor seating.

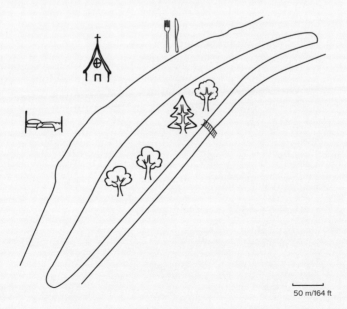

50 m/164 ft

Wheatley's Eyot

This island is partly owned by the Environment Agency, while the rest is owned by the islanders living in the 31 homes. There is a weir at either end, giving islanders the background sound of crashing water. There's evidence of very old human settlements on the island, with artefacts from as long ago as 2000BC discovered in recent decades. One of the weirs was destroyed by a World War I bomb and some locals lost their lives. In more recent years, Wheatley's Ait residents had a run-in with the Environment Agency over access to the island, as the Environment Agency didn't want them using their bridge. After some time, the islanders came to a settlement to pay for access and maintenance of the bridge.

Size and location
Approximate size: 46,500m²
Coordinates: 51.399, -0.415

Can you visit?
No, only Environment Agency employees and islanders can access the island.

Carl's tips:
Have a look at Wheatley's Eyot from the Thames Path, before continuing up towards Walton-on-Thames and the locally loved riverside pubs: The Anglers (Riverside Cottages, Manor Road, KT12 2PF) and The Swan (50 Manor Road, KT12 2PF).

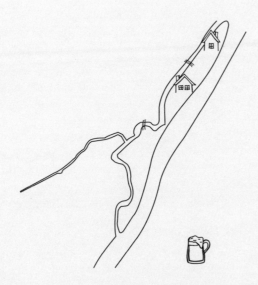

50 m/164 ft

Desborough Island

A large uninhabited, artificially created island, access to Desborough Island is found over two one-way car bridges. The island is named after Lord Desborough, a former chairman of the Thames Conservancy. Nowadays the island has multiple uses. As well as having a water pumping station and large reservoir, it's also home to the University Vandals Rugby Club and the Weybridge Rifle and Pistol Club. By day, locals enjoy the open spaces and woodland areas for walks. The location's funniest claim to fame is that the island and stretch of the River Thames directly surrounding it were used to represent the banks of the Mississippi in the music video for Culture Club's *Karma Chameleon* song.

Size and location
Approximate size: 450,000m²
Coordinates: 51.385, -0.445

Can you visit?
Yes, drive or walk onto the island along Walton Lane.

Carl's tips:
Recreate your own Karma Chameleon moment by taking the 45-minute Shepperton Cruise by JGF Passenger Boats (www.jgfboats.com), which goes past Desborough Island and D'Oyly Carte Island. Another local company, Thames Skiff Hire (www.skiffhire.com) hires out traditional skiffs for several days at a time, for those who want to explore the river and camp as they go.

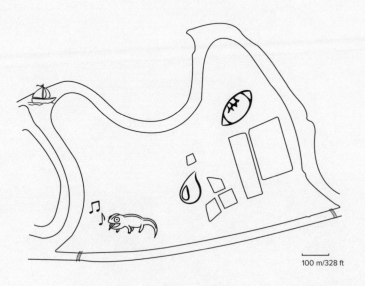

100 m/328 ft

D'Oyly Carte Island

This is a private island with just one grand house, which has 13 bedrooms, six bathrooms and five reception rooms, including a ballroom. Eyot House was built in 1888 by Richard D'Oyly Carte, the producer of the *Gilbert and Sullivan* comic operas. D'Oyly Carte was also the founder of London's Savoy Theatre, the Savoy Hotel and the Palace Theatre. He used the island as a countryside family home – where he is said to have kept a pet crocodile – and W.S. Gilbert and Arthur Sullivan were both previous guests at the house. Access used to be via a chain link ferry, but a metal arched footbridge makes it easier to get to nowadays.

The house has been featured in a number of TV programmes and films over the years. For one programme, the metal footbridge was clad with wood to make it look like the 1940s, for a BBC TV production called *Witness Against Hitler*. Part of the *Alias Smith and Jones* Western series was filmed there too.

The island and house was put up for sale for £4million in 2014 but information about the new owners is still to be announced.

Size and location
Approximate size: 6,500m²
Coordinates: 51.383, -0.454

Can you visit?
No, the island is privately owned.

Carl's tips:
Take a look at D'Oyly Carte Island from the Thames Path on the Weybridge side of the river, where you can walk directly past the entrance to the island's footbridge. Just a short meander away is The Minnow (104 Thames Street, KT13 8NG), a locally loved pub with great food. There's also an unexpectedly brilliant view from the other side of the river, on the corner of Towpath and Ferry Lane.

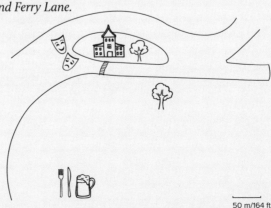

50 m/164 ft

D'OYLY CARTE ISLAND

Lock Island

Shepperton Lock is managed from this island, which is accessible by foot over the lock itself. The island has pleasant areas of greenery and lovely views of the surrounding river.

Size and location:
Approximate size: 17,000m²
Coordinates: 51.382, -0.459

Can you visit?
Yes, just walk over the lock.

Carl's tips:
The lock is also home to the Shepperton Lock Tea Room, which is the ideal spot from which to watch river life passing by.

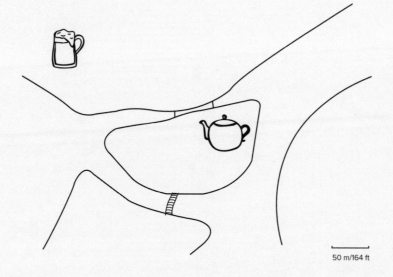

50 m/164 ft

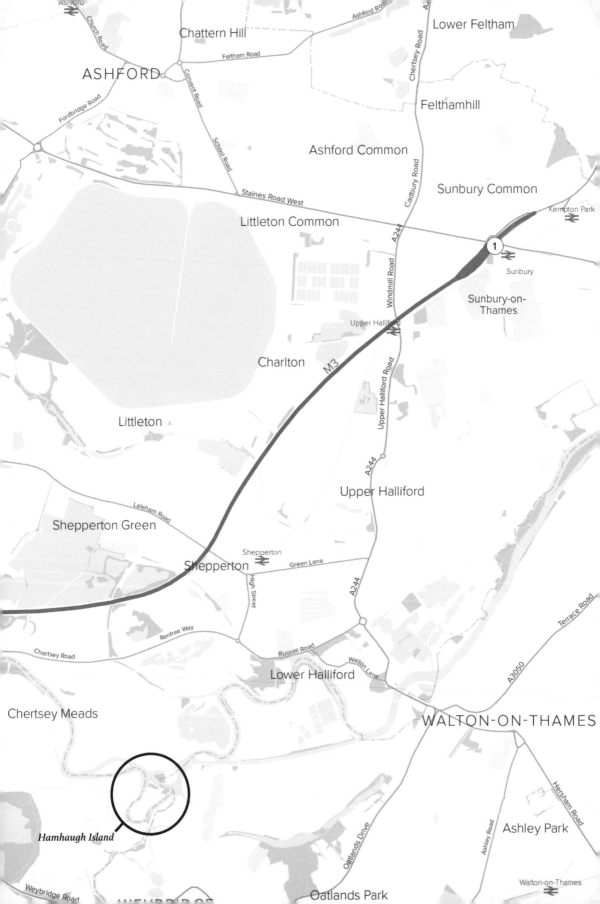

Hamhaugh Island

This residential island is accessed via a footpath surrounded by trees from Lock Island. Nowadays is has around 50 houses and a communal green in the middle, but in the 19th century it was well known as being one of the first islands to be used for summer camping. The island was originally owned by a local boat builder, George Dunton, who rented out plots to campers. These campers arrived from central London in horse drawn vans with their tents and provisions. Families would spend whole summers there, joined only by their menfolk at the weekends, until train services improved and they could commute every day during the summer.

The island was also previously used for hay and a horse ferry used to transport horses and wagons to the island for the peak haymaking season.

A general shop owner, Fred 'Perky' Perkins, started delivering provisions to the island in the 1920s, while an island couple later started selling goods from their shed to weekenders. Also during the 1920s, a toilet used to be in the middle of the island green. The flag could be seen flying high when it was in use!

After Dunton's death, his son took over the business, who decided to sell the camping plots to regular customers. Gradually wooden sheds and chalets were erected in their place. An air raid shelter was added to the green during World War II, when some people started to move to the island permanently to escape the worst of the bombing in London. Some residents reported ducks laying eggs on their boat landings during the war. They were pleased the ducks were also doing their bit for the war effort, as islanders could use these precious eggs in cooking!

One of the island's former residents was Amy Gentry OBE, the pioneer of women's rowing in England. During World War II, she also helped the famous engineer, Barnes Wallis, with his experiments to develop a bouncing bomb. The Gentry family was known as one of the founding families of the island, helping to form the Hamhaugh Islanders' Association, which secured the triangle of land in the centre of the island as communal land.

Electricity was installed on the island in 1948, which is said to have caused much discussion among islanders, some of whom objected to the cost and the interference with their desire for a simpler way of life.

There is a thriving although private island community today and regular social events are held on the central green.

Size and location:
Approximate size: 44,000m^2
Coordinates: 51.380, -0.460

Can you visit?
No, access is for residents only.

Carl's tips:
The best place to spot Hamhaugh Island is from the Weybridge Point car park (114 Thames Street, KT13 8NG). Look out for the weir, which islanders cross to get onto the island.

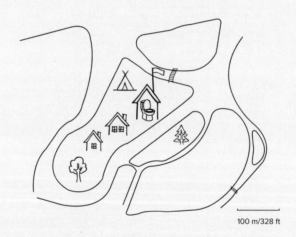

100 m/328 ft

HAMHAUGH ISLAND

Tegwynne Goldthorpe
Architect

Having built her own house on Hamhaugh Island, architect Tegwynne loves the community spirit and active lifestyle that living on an island brings.

How did you discover Hamhaugh Island?

I always wanted to live by the river because I went on Hoseasons boat holidays as a kid with my parents. I always remember looking at the passing scenery and thinking I wanted to live in one of the houses with a lawn that led down to the river. I've always wanted to build my own house too. The first riverside plot I bought was on the mainland in Shepperton. It just had a shack on it at the time and so I built a new house in its place. I started getting more work in the local area and then got a client who lived on Hamhaugh Island. I thought the island was lovely, but wasn't sure I could ever make the transition of not being able to drive right up to my house. Around the same time, I was looking for a new project and another old shack was for sale. It happened to be on Hamhaugh Island, on a plot that is the southernmost point of the River Thames. I bought it in the early 2000s.

What were your first months on Hamhaugh Island like?

I had to live in the old shack for several months until I got planning permission. It was freezing cold and half the roof was missing – which wasn't great, as it was constantly raining at the time. But I struggled through it. Then I had my new house built on the plot – project managing and buying every single thing for it. I've never looked back. I have a true love of the river and creating my own house in this location was fantastic.

Tell us about your work.

I'm an architect and I worked for different firms for a number of years before setting up my own practice in 2000. It's one of the best things I've ever done – I love working for myself. My work varies between the bread and butter of doing house extensions and loft conversions, to doing the nicer riverside houses. I used to do quite a lot of restaurant work as well, but now I'm enjoying the riverside houses most, even though the planning regulations are very difficult. I've always loved my work. It's always a joy to meet different people and design something they want, that fits the character of the site.

Describe the practical side of living on Hamhaugh Island.

Being on a footbridge-only island, residents have a long walk from their cars to their houses. Everyone has a trolley for transporting things and there's a lot of trolley envy when someone gets a bigger or better one! It's very difficult for the fire brigade to get here if there's a problem, so we have water pumps and regular fire drills. We're not allowed to have fireworks or bonfires during the spring and summer. But we're a close community and everyone embraces getting together for things like this. Living here means you have to respect the river. I take my daughter to school by boat every day. There are some days when the river's running too high or fast, so we have to take the car instead. It takes five minutes by boat but up to an hour to get there and back by car because of traffic. Living on the water can be really convenient, but also inconvenient at times.

How have you been affected by flooding?

There have been two bad floods since I've lived on the island. Our garden was flooded both times, but all our electricity and plumbing continued working. However, it was difficult to get off the island. We had to use waders all the way up the lane towards Shepperton. We took the dogs in a kayak up to higher ground so they could run around. It was like something out of a movie. A lot of people left the island during these times – not necessarily because their houses were flooded, but because they had to get to work. Those who stayed were quite isolated. I always thought the mooring posts by our jetty were really tall, but now we know how high the water can get.

Describe the social side of island life.

Even during the tougher times of flooding, people generally make the best of everything. In the summer, it takes you forever to get off the island because you talk to everybody on your way and get stuck chatting. We have a social committee that organises a number of events over the year. We've had everything from Christmas carols, cocktail nights and barn dances, to kids' fun days, plant sales and island games. We always participate in the local raft race too. We also have occasional croquet matches and invite some of the other local islanders across. The island is a great place to host parties – all our non-islander friends love it when we have them over.

What's it like bringing up a family on the island?

We've had various families here. Some love it; others find it difficult. It's particularly hard for those who have a few children who constantly need to be driven to different functions. Always walking on and off the island to take them places can become a bit of a bind. But the trade-off is that you get to bring them up in such a gorgeous place. As everyone knows each other, they can run around and visit each other's houses. You have to teach children to be respectful of the river from the beginning, but as they get older, they can really enjoy it. My daughter regularly swims in the river and loves it.

Has your lifestyle changed since you've lived on an island?

I started rowing. We've got several local rowing clubs and I would watch people row past, thinking I wouldn't be any good at it. But years of cycling and running really helped me and I really enjoy it. The rowing community is lovely. Amy Gentry OBE – a pioneer of women's rowing in England – used to live on Hamhaugh Island, so it's also very fitting to be involved in rowing here.

What's the best thing about living on Hamhaugh Island?

The location is great – you can take the boat across and be in Shepperton, Weybridge or Hampton Court really quickly. It's very quiet, except for the occasional church bells from Weybridge and the white noise of water from the weirs at night. It's so quick to catch the train into central London too. When I cross over the bridges in London, it's a lovely thought that the very same water has passed my house.

Find out more about Tegwynne Goldthorpe at www.tegwynne-goldthorpe.co.uk

HAMHAUGH ISLAND

Rosina Lyford
Artist

Acclaimed international artist Rosina discovered Hamhaugh Island by accident, and is now one of the longest-standing residents.

How did you discover Hamhaugh Island?

It's a weird story. I'd saved up around £3,000 through my work, which was an enormous amount of money in the 1970s. I thought to myself: 'I've never had an E-Type Jaguar'. It was a totally impractical thought, but I bought a copy of *Exchange and Mart* magazine to look for a car. Instead, I saw an advert that said 'House on island for sale.' The cost was the value of my house plus my savings. I found the idea so intriguing, I just had to go and look at the house.

What made you decide to buy the house?

The young girl who took me for the house viewing said that as soon as we arrived on the island, she could see from my face I was going to buy the house. It was love at first sight, simple as that. I hadn't gone out to look for a house and I wasn't so rich that I could make decisions like that without a financial impact. Everyone on the island thought I was a very rich and stupid artist because I wouldn't have surveyors or lawyers look at it, as I knew it wouldn't have passed any inspections. I instantly loved the place and I just wanted it. So I sold my house and moved in within six weeks. It was meant to be.

What did your friends and family think about you moving to the island?

My sons didn't want to live here. They were coming up to university age and they wanted to be in central London, and I wanted to be further out. I told them it was tough luck. They'd be off living with friends after university anyway and I wanted to be on the island. There was no running water when I first moved in; just a standpipe that ran down the middle of the island. When I told my parents I was moving from a nice modern house in Richmond to a wooden house on an island with no running water, they thought I was mad!

What are your early memories of living on the island?

One very cold winter morning, I wondered what I'd done; I thought I was going to freeze to death. It reminded me of the band called Three Dog Night. I only had one dog, and I remember pulling him onto the bed because it was so cold, I needed his body heat. He'd never been on the bed before. He looked at me as if I'd gone completely crazy! I think you've got to be a little bit off-the-wall to live here.

Tell us about your work.

I'm a working artist who has exhibited internationally, particularly in Norway and New York. My work has also been sold to a number of private collectors, particularly in Germany. My style is figurative and my paintings are now spread across the world. I was at the height of my career around the time I moved to Hamhaugh Island. After a while, working with galleries in other countries became unreliable and I decided to focus on work closer to home. The exhibition I'm most proud of is the Internasjonal KUNST-utstilling in 1988. It was an exhibition where my work was shown alongside that of Chagall, Kemal, Carcan, Rosseland, Adami, Miro, Picasso, Moore, Hauki, Bazinet and Chemiakin. I'm the only surviving artist of all of them.

How does the island inspire your work?

The quietness is profound. I need space to dream to do my work, and the island gives that to me. I've got to draw inspiration from somewhere, and if it's busy all the time, there's no space in me to find it. Hopefully I pass this sense of wonder on in the form of images, rhythm and colour in my work.

How does the island hit your senses?

I can smell the water when I walk across the weir. Every single day that I walk on and off the island, I notice the smell of the water. No two days are the same. Many buildings on the island are made of wood, so things expand and contract. Everything creaks. On the island, I'm incredibly aware of all the noises, the colours and the changes of the seasons. Having no roads on the island is an utter delight. When I lie in bed – even though it can be freezing cold – the only thing I can hear are the wild geese flying over the top. The darkness on the island is beautiful too – we don't have very much of it in life nowadays. When I first arrived on the island, I would lay on my lawn and watch the night skies and shooting stars.

What tends to bring people to live on Hamhaugh Island?

The island is a Marmite place; people either love it or hate it. I'm always pleased to see people settle in well and become islanders. A love of the water is the thing that brings most people to the island. I like to swim in the river. But if you don't respect the water, you don't live here. It has its moods! We have exciting times with occasional flooding, but a couple of floods have been a bit too exciting. When the water goes down again, you can't believe it ever happened. A friend visited me on the island after a bad flooding event, looked around, and said it didn't look like the flood had been that bad. Then I pointed to a boat that had got stuck on some mooring posts almost three metres in the air!

Is there any light relief for islanders during the times of bad flooding?

Despite the hardship, there are some lovely island stories from times of flooding. One of the islanders likes to collect things. During an episode of flooding, he thought someone had stolen all the empty glass bottles he had stacked in front of his house. In fact, his gate had been left open, and all the bottles had floated down to the island green like ducks! Another islander, Mike, lost his electricity during a flood, so he couldn't make anything hot to eat. One of his neighbours, David, had flooding inside the house, but he did have electricity. So David invited Mike over for a stew one evening. Mike turned up wearing a fancy shirt, a cravat and a proper jacket – but with waders on, while David was cooking in the kitchen wearing his wellies! They sat in the kitchen and had a posh stew and a bottle of wine. I thought it was a lovely attitude.

What's the social side of Hamhaugh Island like?

We have lots of social events, which are very important in a small community. If there's an emergency, we have to work together, so social events are important to cement the community. They're jollies with a purpose, but our events are a lot of fun too.

Do you enjoy the wildlife on the island?

There's so much going on with the wildlife – big and small – on the island. One of my favourite wildlife events was when an islander rescued a tiny Muscovy duckling who had lost its mother. The only way she could think to keep it warm and alive was to put it in with her rabbit, so she tucked the duckling under the rabbit's arm. This male rabbit looked disgusted, but nevertheless did what his owner wanted and the duckling grew into an adult. We taught it to swim, and off it went. The next year, the same duck came back with lots of its own ducklings. Amazingly, the duck took all its ducklings into the rabbit's cage and laid there with her wing over them all, including the rabbit. You've never seen a rabbit that looked more fed up, but it was a wonderful thing to watch!

What advice would you give to someone hoping to live on an island?

Living on an island sounds lovely and sweet, but you've got to be quite practical and independent because it can be hard work. I don't think there's a man or woman on this island who isn't capable of almost building their own house! A lot of people think moving to an island is a dream to have for your old age, but I think it would be quite a hard transition when you're older. So if you're going to do it, get here by at least the age of 50, unless you're very fit.

Would you ever leave the island?

I occasionally get what I call 'small island blues'. I do need the city sometimes, so I go to central London for a bit of buzz. I love the theatres and galleries. But I wouldn't want to live there anymore; I just need to go in for my quick fix. I need to live by the water. It makes reflections on my walls that change throughout the day. One day, I felt very uncomfortable in my house, and I couldn't work out why. I went outside and realised the river had frozen over! It caused the patterns on my walls to stop. The experience of the water is an important part of the feeling I have on the island. People think I'm mad when they ask me what I've done all day, and I say I've been watching the patterns on the walls. But I tell them it's really important – if I don't watch the world, it might stop. Somebody's got to do it!

Have you made any fascinating discoveries about former islanders?

Felicity Kendal CBE used to live on the island. She had a fascinating life as she was brought up in India; her father ran a Shakespeare company there. They travelled from place to place across the country to perform. I met her father on the island once and he was absolutely flamboyant, sweeping down the island with his cape and hat. Felicity was married to Drewe Henley at the time, who was in *Star Wars* and *The Avengers*. The island has always had a strong connection with rowing too, since the female rowing pioneer Amy Gentry OBE – and other female rowers – lived here. During my time on the island, some of these former rowers would pick up others from their retirement homes and bring them to the island for get-togethers. I'd walk past them painting a fence or doing some other odd jobs – all aged in their 90s – smoking like chimneys and telling dirty stories!

anworth

try Way

npton Pa

ast

A3050

157

Pharaoh's Island

A residential island of 23 homes with Egyptian-inspired names, Pharaoh's Island is only accessible by boat. There's a story that says the island was presented to Admiral Nelson in 1798 after the Battle of the Nile, although there's no evidence of this being the case. The Nelson connection to the area is more likely due to him being a keen fisherman in the area.

The island had a variety of permanent bungalows and wooden weekend chalets until the 1980s, when larger brick structures became the norm. Among other previously famous residents, actor Ian Hendry from *The Avengers* fame and his wife Janet Munro from the *Swiss Family Robinson* lived there.

Previous residents also report an eclectic bunch of former neighbours. One is said to have regularly fired his pistol at the plates on his wife's dresser; while a resident ferryman is said to have drilled a hole in a rival ferryman's boat, so it would sink with him in it.

A path runs through the centre of the island and there's a large green for social events for islanders.

Size and location
Approximate size: 16,500m²
Coordinates: 51.382, -0.465

Can you visit?
No, only islanders can gain access.

Carl's tips:
Walk along the Thames Path on the Shepperton side of the river to get a perfect look at the gorgeous houses on Pharaoh's Island. The Thames Court (Towpath, TW17 9LJ) is about halfway between Pharaoh's Island and Hamhaugh Island on the riverbank, making it the perfect spot to stop for a drink or a bite to eat.

50 m/164 ft

Emma Muir
Business owner

As the owner of a house on Pharaoh's Island that hosted wild pool parties visited by Jimi Hendrix, Emma loves the island's history and ever-changing riverside life.

How did you discover Pharaoh's Island?

I was living in central London near Tower Bridge when I met my partner Andrew, who was living in Surbiton. One day, we took my sons out on Andrew's boat, travelling through London on the River Thames. We were all amazed by the houses that had gardens going directly to the river, so much so that when Andrew and I moved in together, we knew we really wanted to live on the river. So we started looking for houses. We wanted to be a little bit outside of London, but still commutable for work. We came to view three houses up for sale on Pharaoh's Island and completely fell in love with the house we're in now, Sphinx. It was out of budget at the time, but we were given the opportunity to rent the house for six months before deciding. We couldn't bring ourselves to leave after the six months were up, so we made the budget work and bought it. That was in 2012, and we haven't looked back since.

Describe the feeling of living on Pharaoh's Island.

It's like being in a wildlife park in the middle of nowhere, without actually being in the middle of nowhere. We're still in the outer London area just a short distance from the train station, motorways, the airport, and Shepperton village or Weybridge for the shops. It's very quiet, except for the sound of the nearby weir, the occasional plane and summertime boat parties. Everyone who lives here loves it. People who love the water can do any activity from their house too, from kayaking to paddle boarding. Whenever I come home across the river, I get a moment of complete peace and tranquillity.

Tell us about your work.

I run my own business, an agency supplying part-time marketing staff for tech businesses who don't need full time marketing personnel. Now I run the business from my office on Pharaoh's Island, which is wonderful. Some days I commute into London to meet clients and other days I'm in my office, which is in a separate building from the house.

What do you like about working from Pharaoh's Island?

There's no need to have an office in the city anymore and I like the fact it saves me the slog of having to go into London on a regular basis. I tend to start work very early and it's so easy to get up and walk a few paces to my office on the island. It's very quiet here. I have birdfeeders right outside the office attracting all kinds of birds and sometimes the ducks tap on the office door to remind me to feed them! If I have a spare five minutes, I go to my vegetable patch or greenhouse to do a bit of weeding. My office is right next to our swimming pool too, which looks very inviting during the summer. Working from the island is fantastic, but I have to be disciplined, since there are so many distractions.

What makes people want to live on an island?

You have to be a certain kind of person. I wouldn't call us quirky as we're all quite normal, but something has happened in islanders' lives that makes them want to do something different. Although we find living on an island easy, you have to be someone who has an adventurous streak. Often the river is calm, but when it's really flowing, it's a more challenging way of life. Many people here want to get away from the commotion of central London too, but they don't want to be too far away either.

What kind of people live on Pharaoh's Island?

Everyone on the island is very different. Our oldest resident is 92, but we also have families with younger children. Some people have been here for 50 years or more, while newcomers have come in to fix up some of the older houses. Some are retired, others work locally or in London. In terms of professions, we've got everyone from project managers and solicitors, to interior designers and singers. It's a real mix of people but we all get on.

Tell us about the community spirit.

It's the first place I've lived where I've known and socialised with all my neighbours. On the day we moved in, everyone got together in their boats and helped us move our stuff over. If anyone's boat breaks down, we help each other out. We organise several social events a year – many of them on our communal green – but there are plenty of impromptu occasions too, where people invite one another over for a drink. It's the friendliest place I've ever lived. Every Christmas we do a big boat display, where we all decorate our boats – the more exotic the better – and parade around the island a few times. Then we get together for Christmas carols and mulled wine. It's an annual tradition that's been going on for years. Along with many of the other islands, we also participate in the Shepperton Village Fair Raft Race. We've won it for the last few years – it helps that one of our residents is a retired set designer!

What's the best thing about living on the island?

My favourite discovery is finding out that swans mate for life. A pair of swans return annually to the same nest in our garden to lay eggs. They diligently sit on them for 45 days and nights and then nurture their young for up to 10 months, before letting them go off and join the other teenage swan groups. Our pair of swans visit daily for food in the winter too, and in the summer they bring the cygnets to our orchard to rest in the shade. We see the whole cycle every year and feel very much part of it. Everything about living on the river is absolutely fantastic. You can look out of the window every single day and the view is always different. It inspires me. It doesn't matter if it's absolutely pouring down with rain. Even when we had the terrible floods in 2014, it didn't put us off.

What was life like during the floods?

We lived in waders for two weeks! Our whole garden was under water; the river was flowing straight through it. We had to kayak from our back door to the jetty to get on the boat. We were working in London at the time, so we had to take the boat to the lock, then wade up to our car and drive to the train station. It was quite bizarre to start the day in waders, take them off to reveal our suits underneath, then go into the centre of London. If only people knew how our days had started! Every evening during the floods, we got together in one of the islanders' houses to check everyone was ok and make a plan in case we needed to evacuate some of the older residents. There was great camaraderie. We'd open a bottle of champagne and laugh together. All the press helicopters were flying overhead and we could do was stand there and wave.

What's the most difficult thing about living on an island?

There are some practical things you have to be aware of. For example, the fire brigade can't get here, and although there is a boat fire brigade, it would take them some time to get here in an emergency. So we have our own pumps on the island and do regular fire training. Some other services can't get to the island, like ambulances, so we have to take people over to them on the riverbank in those situations. The water company once wanted to come and change our meter, but when we went to pick them up on the riverbank, they said they weren't allowed to get on the boat for health and safety reasons! But we've never had a problem getting anything onto the island. We got my baby grand piano, a hot tub and 70 tonnes of stone for our patio over with no problem.

How do people react when you tell them you live on an island?

Some friends think I'm absolutely crazy. When people visit us, they understand why we love it, but most say they'd never do it themselves. The boat journey is a mental block for many people, even though it only takes 30 seconds to get across. Some of my clients think it's funny that I start my day on a boat before getting the train to see them in London! The reactions are very polarised and when people come to the island to look at properties for sale, it's either not for them and they never come back, or they fall in love with it.

What have you discovered about the history of your house?

Sphinx was the first house on the island, built in 1903 by an Egyptologist. He owned the island and gradually sold off other plots to fund his trips to Egypt. In the 1960s, the first Disney actress Janet Munro and *The Avengers* actor Ian Hendry lived here. We've got some wonderful photos of them living in the house and arriving here after their wedding. They lived here for a number of years and according to our old neighbour Peggy, they had a lot of wild pool parties. Apparently Jimi Hendrix once swam in our pool! Peggy used to be invited to the parties. The reason we had a hot tub installed is because Peggy told us Janet and Ian used to have one in exactly the same spot by the pool.

Your neighbour Peggy sounds like a great person to know.

She's incredible. Unfortunately she had to move off the island at the age of 87 because of her knees, but before she left she was still rowing every day. She had lived on the island since 1943 and bought the house from her father to live in with her husband. Every time we saw her she had a new story for us, whether it was about the Thames freezing over so you could walk to the towpath, to all the shoes Janet Munro used to give her!

You were also involved in the filming of Queen and Country – tell us about that.

The director John Boorman filmed part of *Queen and Country* – which was the sequel to *Hope and Glory* – in our garden. The films were semi-autobiographical of his experiences during and after the war, when he spent time with family in one of the houses near ours. They reconstructed our house itself in a studio in Romania, but they filmed some scenes in our garden, albeit with some modifications so it looked like the 1950s. There was a film crew of around 60 people here for a week. Andrew was an extra and did some boat camera operator work for them too. It was great fun!

What's the most unexpected local discovery you've made since living on Pharaoh's Island?

The local Indian restaurant delivery driver knows exactly when to phone us on his way over, so we can meet him in the boat on the jetty. We enjoy piping hot curry every time we order!

Penton Hook Lock Island and Penton Hook Island

The small lock island near the riverbank has just a lock keeper's hut and a little greenery. However, walking across it leads to the much larger, artificially constructed Penton Hook Island, found in a large oxbow bend in the River Thames. In the 1600s it was a burial ground for victims of the Great Plague; later it was used for haymaking. Nowadays it's a protected nature reserve, popular with anglers and curious picnickers. It is at risk of the occasional flood, hence why there are no permanent residences there.

Size and location:
Approximate size: 4,000m²
Coordinates: 51.413, -0.501

Can you visit?
Yes, walk across the lock.

Carl's tips:
Walk along the Thames Path on the Staines side of the river to get a view of the island and access to the lock. A short walk away is The Retreat (Staines Road, TW18 2RT), a gastropub and perfect spot for a drink.

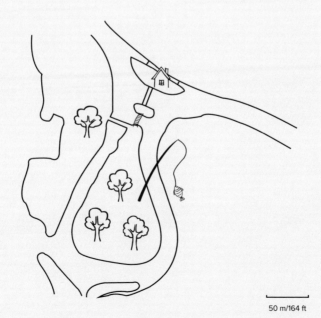

50 m/164 ft

Truss's Island

This small uninhabited island is accessible by two wooden footbridges. The island is named after Charles Truss who improved the navigability of the River Thames by implementing a series of improvements to both locks and towpaths. This had a positive knock-on effect, allowing more trade to take place along the river. Nowadays, the island is a pretty, landscaped riverside park with fishing platforms, picnic areas, benches, a temporary mooring and wildlife feeding steps.

Size and location:
Approximate size: 1,400m²
Coordinates: 51.419, -0.513

Can you visit?
Yes, just walk across the footbridges.

Carl's tips:
Walk onto the island from the Thorpe side of the river, or catch a glimpse of it from the Thames Path on the other riverbank.

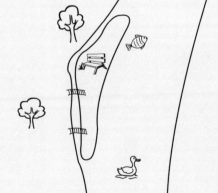

20 m/66 ft

TRUSS'S ISLAND

Church Island

This inhabited island with just six houses is connected to the mainland by a footbridge, hidden by foliage that is dense in places. Some historians believe the island was crossed by a Roman bridge, making a waypoint on the Devil's Highway route to Londinium.

Size and location:
Approximate size: 9,500m²
Coordinates: 51.435, -0.520

Can you visit?
No, access is for islanders only.

Carl's tips:
Catch a glimpse of the island from Church Street, or look at it from the Thames Path on the other side of the river.

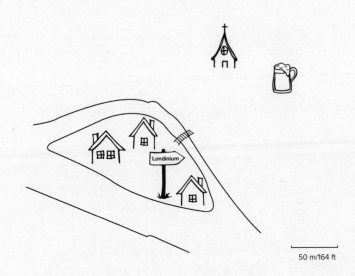

50 m/164 ft

Holm Island

This narrow island has just one house on it called The Nest, which sits more or less in the middle. This was the island used as a hideaway by the future King Edward VIII, where he courted Mrs Wallis Simpson during the 1930s. It's connected to the mainland via a metal footbridge.

Size and location:
Approximate size: 12,000m^2
Coordinates: 51.436, -0.529

Can you visit?
No, access is for the private owner only.

Carl's tips:
Catch a glimpse of the island from the Thames Path on the Surrey riverbank, although it's difficult to tell it's an island sometimes due to thick foliage. The Runnymede on Thames Hotel & Spa (Windsor Road, Egham TW20 0AG; www.runnymedehotel.com) nearby rents out boats by the hour or day during the spring and summer, which are ideal for getting a closer look at these nearby islands.

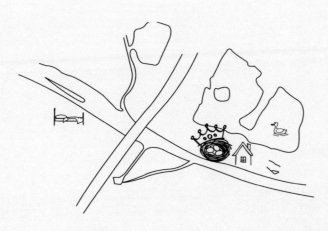

100 m/328 ft

The Island

Connected to the mainland by a road bridge, this island is simply known as The Island and is home to around 20 families.

Size and location:
Approximate size: 18,000m²
Coordinates: 51.442, -0.547

Can you visit?
No, access is for islanders only.

Carl's tips:
Have a look at The Island from the Thames Path on the Surrey riverbank. Continue along the path to reach the Runnymede Pleasure Grounds, ideal for picnics and drinking in the view on this perfect bend in the river. The French Brothers boat company (www.frenchbrothers. co.uk) runs boat trips from here to Windsor, ideal for taking in all the islands on the way.

100 m/328 ft

Magna Carta Island

This uninhabited island is thought to be the place where King John sealed the Magna Carta in 1215, although the exact location in the local area is hotly contested. The charter was to establish peace between the unpopular King and a group of rebellious barons. The Magna Carta is widely seen as the first step towards democracy. As a result, this whole area surrounding the island is globally symbolic.

The island was previously owned by an old Benedictine nunnery, St Mary's Priory and you can still spot the ruins today from the side of the river the Thames Path side runs along. In later years, this is the place that Henry III (later Louis VIII of France) used for meetings, and where Henry VIII is said to have courted Ann Boleyn. The Ankerwycke yew – the National Trust's oldest tree at 2,500 years old – is nearby too.

George Harcourt, the lord of a local manor, built a gothic cottage on the island in the 1830s. He installed the Charta Stone – a stone slab commemorating the sealing of the Magna Carta. The island has been owned and leased by a range of fascinating characters ever since, including an MP, Sir Patrick Hannon, and Miss Alberto Catherine Bigelow, an American author. The Queen even visited in 1974 to plant a tree in the garden.

Magna Carta Island and the house on it were put up for sale for £3.95 million in 2014. The new owner occasionally rents out rooms in the house on Airbnb.

Size and location:
Approximate size: 73,750m²
Coordinates: 51.444, -0.557

Can you visit?
No, access is for the island's owner only.

Carl's tips:
The walk along the Thames Path on the Runnymede riverbank feels like a lost piece of England, although it's hard to distinguish any features on the heavily wooded Magna Carta Island closer to the other riverbank. Although it's not possible to get onto Magna Carta Island itself, get the feeling of the locality by visiting the National Trust (www.nationaltrust. org.uk) sites nearby. In particular, The Park circular walk at Ankerwycke is an easy walk for all abilities.

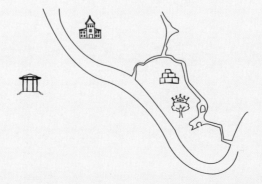

100 m/328 ft

MAGNA CARTA ISLAND

Pat's Croft Eyot

This is a private island with one house on it and various boats moored to it. Its inhabitants reach the island by boat or by using the sweet wooden footbridge.

Size and location:
Approximate size: 3,850m²
Coordinates: 51.449, -0.566

Can you visit?
No, access is for the island's inhabitants only.

Carl's tips:
You can get a great view of the island from the Thames Path by The Runnymede Boathouse. Afterwards, cross the road for a cup of tea in the National Trust tearoom, before crossing the ancient fields to the Magna Carta Monument, John F Kennedy Memorial and The Jurors artwork.

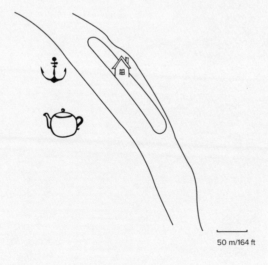

50 m/164 ft

Kingfisher Island

This small island has just three houses on it and is attached to the mainland by a footbridge.

Size and location:

Approximate size: 2,500m^2
Coordinates: 51.454, -0.573

Can you visit?

No, access is for the island's inhabitants only.

Carl's tips:

Have a peek of Kingfisher Island from the Thames Path on the Old Windsor side of the river.

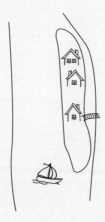

20 m/66 ft

Friary Island

Barely looking like an island given the tiniest channel of water running alongside it, Friary Island is attached to the mainland by a road bridge. There are around 50 houses and businesses on the island.

Size and location:

Approximate size: 40,000m²
Coordinates: 51.458, -0.573

Can you visit?

Yes, just follow the public road called Friary Island.

Carl's tips:

A short drive away is Wraysbury village and the 600 year old pub, The George Inn (29 Windsor Road, TW19 5DE).

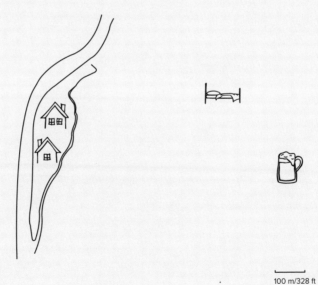

100 m/328 ft

Friday Island

This tiny wooded island is near Old Windsor Lock. It has just one two-bedroom cottage on it. The island's most notable claim to fame is that it is the former residence of the forensic scientist and intelligence officer, Dr Julius Grant. Dr Grant famously proved the Hitler Diaries published in *The Sunday Times* were forgeries. He used to describe rowing over to his island to feel like he was going a million miles away. The current owners of the island use it as an occasional holiday home.

Size and location:
Approximate size: 100m²
Coordinates: 51.4625, -0.5692

Can you visit?
No, the island is privately owned.

Carl's tips:
The Thames Path on the Old Windsor side of the river offers the perfect view of Friday Island.

20 m/66 ft

Colnbro[...]

The Queen Mother
Reservoir

Windsor Road

London Road

Datchet

Ditton Road

Datchet

Horton Road

Horton

Southlea Road

Sunnymeads

Welley Road

Road

A308

Old Windsor

Old Windsor Lock Island

St Luke's Road

Straight Road

Windsor Road   Wraysbury

Wraysbury

Wra[...]
Res[...]

Burfield Road

A328   A308

Staines Road   Staines Road

Priest Hill

Hythe End   Wraysbury Road

13

A30

Ch[...]

Bishopsgate

Windsor Road

Runnymede

A30

St Jude's Road

Egham By-Pass

A308   The Caus[...]

A30

EGHAM

Pooley
Green

Egham H[...]

Egham Hill

Egham

Vicarage Road

Englefield Green

A328

Royal Holloway

Thorpe Lea Road

Old Windsor Lock Island

This island is attached to the mainland by the lock itself and is home to the lock keeper's cottage, woodland and a few moored boats. A weir also connects the island to Ham Island next door.

Size and location:
Approximate size: 4,000m²
Coordinates: 51.463, -0.569

Can you visit?
No, only people using the lock or accessing the moorings can visit the island.

Carl's tips:
Have a look at the lock from the Thames Path, before going off to explore Old Windsor nearby. Pubs include The Fox & Castle (21 Burfield Road, SL4 2RB) and The Oxford Blue (10 Crimp Hill, SL4 2QY), dating back to at least the 1700s and 1800s respectively.

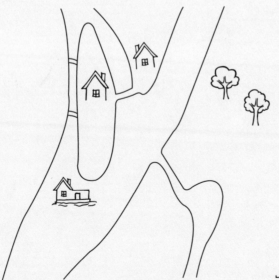

20 m/66 ft

Ham Island

A large, inhabited, man-made island, Ham Island is one of the larger islands on the river. It was created when the river's course was diverted to allow an easier river route to Windsor. The properties on the island were originally holiday homes, many of which have been redeveloped into more luxurious accommodation for around 100 islanders nowadays. Heavy flooding in 2014 led to some people abandoning their homes and a horse rescue centre was evacuated. A reference to Ham Island is made in *Three Men in a Boat*, where they note they can see Windsor Castle from this point in the river. Two significant areas of Ham Island are covered by a Scheduled Ancient Monument, since it includes the site of Edward the Confessor's Palace and the early medieval and medieval palace of Kingsbury.

Size and location:
Approximate size: 508,750m²
Coordinates: 51.470, -0.568

Can you visit?
Yes, just follow Ham Lane over the road bridge.

Carl's tips:
Get a good view of Ham Island from the Thames Path, or enjoy an alternative view from The Avenue in Sunnymeads.

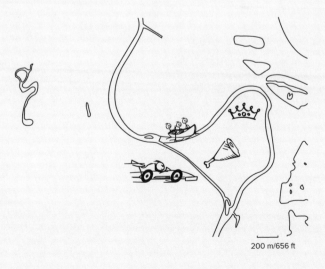

200 m/656 ft

Gordon Spice
Former British racing driver

Racing car driver and entrepreneur Gordon gained recognition across the world during his career, but his home on Ham Island has always been a welcome retreat.

Introduce yourself.

I was a professional racing driver and during my career, I had contracts with BMC, Ford and General Motors, among many others. I drove everything from sports cars to Formula 5000, in locations across the world. I also started the first car cash and carry business in the UK, which went national with branches all over the country. I had an engineering company too, which produced racing cars. We had factories at Silverstone and in Atlanta in the USA, where we had a contract with General Motors. Recently, there's been a revival of old cars and wealthy people are buying and racing them. I've been selling some of my old trophies with the cars, which adds enormous value to them. I won around 150 trophies in total – which was great – but they're also a real pain to clean, house and generally look after! After selling a few, I've now got it down to a more manageable 50.

How did you discover Ham Island?

My wife Mandy and I were living in a small cottage near Virginia Water. We decided we wanted to live on the water, near my office in Staines. We hired a boat and went up and down the river looking for houses. We spotted a house on Ham Island for sale, which was a lot cheaper than other houses we were looking at. The island was completely wild at that time. It took some convincing to move here, but the proximity to Heathrow Airport was also a draw for us. At the time, I was frequently flying long haul for racing, from Japan one week to the west coast of the US the next. So we moved to Ham Island in 1978 and have been here ever since.

Describe the island.

The island has a road bridge, so you wouldn't really know you're on an island. We see ourselves more as being part of Old Windsor village. However, some work was done on the bridge recently and it was closed for several hours each day. That made us realise a bit more that we're on an island. Ham Island is in a very convenient location, whether you want to go to Heathrow Airport, into London or onto the motorways outside of London. We get some aircraft noise given the proximity to the airport, but it's getting noticeably quieter all the time. The next generation of aircraft will have their engines above the wings, and the ones after that will be electric, so they won't be heard at all. A real mixture of people live on the island; we've had families from other countries, actors and those involved in theatre. Everybody gets on. There are about 50 houses altogether, as well as some fields and horse riding stables. Many houses have views of the water and a mooring.

Do you go out on the water?

We've got a little boat we go out on in the evening sometimes, along with a bag of ice and some drinks. We got the boat after I retired. It's a rigid raiding craft as used by the Royal Marines – we went down to Poole to watch it being built. Our friends had visions that our boat would be a huge gin palace! But we wanted to be close to the water so we can see everything.

Have you had any issues with flooding?

The rivers aren't dredged anymore because of concerns from environmentalists, but ever since this stopped, there have been problems with flooding. The last flood was in 2014, when water came halfway up our lawn and we needed waders to leave the house. The side of the island we live on is slightly higher than the other side, where people had up to a metre of water inside their houses. A lot of those houses had to be rebuilt. Since then, we've also noticed how few ducks and swans are around, because a lot of the eggs were washed away during the floods.

How do you get most enjoyment out of the location?

It's a great place if you're a nature watcher. I've become one since living here; that's something the river's done for us. Parakeets come along and take fruit off the apple tree. We've got a regular kingfisher that sits outside – I watch him out the window every morning. We occasionally spot salmon during spawning season. The purity of the water has really improved over the years. We've had the occasional deer too. If they fall in the river at Windsor Great Park, this is the first section of river where they can get out, which we've seen happening a few times.

What else is there on Ham Island?

The island has a sewage works, which doesn't sound very nice, but it's very well run and we never smell anything. Interestingly, the sewage works were created when Albert married Victoria and came to live in England in the 19th century. Coming from Germany, where they had flushing lavatories, Albert was horrified the standards weren't the same at Windsor Castle, where they threw their waste out of the windows into the moat. So he had the sewage works built on Ham Island, which exclusively serviced Windsor Castle in those days. Albert also put in a number of locks and weirs on the River Thames to control water flow. He's responsible for having the new cut dug out that created Ham Island, called so because it's shaped like a joint of ham.

What other historical stories have you discovered about Ham Island?

The fields on Ham Island are part of an ancient monument and the former site of Edward the Confessor's Palace. This area was the original Windsor, and the Windsor as it's known today was called New Windsor. So this is actually a much more historic site. It's also an archaeological site. This means metal detectors can't

be used and when we have the fields harvested, the local farmer can't dig further than a plough's depth – which is around 25cm – because it could disturb old artefacts. Should anything be found, we would have to hand it in by law. We've built a few houses on the island and every time we dig anything, the archaeologists have to come along to observe.

Tell us about what you've built on the island.

I retired quite early in 1989, so I needed something to keep me busy! I already owned some of the fields and we'd already done some building work on the island by that point. All the original plots were quite narrow making it difficult to build decently sized houses, so I had the original track moved to help improve this. It took me 10 years to get planning permission with lots of conditions attached due to the archaeological site, but doing so enabled us to build a few houses. We sold some and rent others. We sold one older house to a man who said he'd fallen in love with it, but he turned out to be a property developer. He had the whole house knocked down and I found myself trying to salvage bits of furniture from the house that I'd built!

Have you made any other changes to the island?

I put in a proper road for access – previously it was a mud track. We brought in mains water to the island, as before that the island just had 10 holiday homes serviced with a plastic hose! I also undergrounded the electricity supply so the telegraph poles could be removed, brought in mains gas and installed automated security gates.

What are you working on at the moment?

I've introduced a sign to the road on the island with a speed limit. We get delivery drivers speeding along in their huge vans at 40mph, which is unsafe because there are children and animals on the island. I'm on a mission about it, which is quite ironic, given what I used to do for a living!

What's the story behind the name of your house?

It's called Bear Shack. The former owner was a gynaecologist called Edward or 'Teddy'. He was a keen naturist and used to host nude parties here. So the name Bear Shack is a pun on his name and what used to go on here!

Would you ever leave the island?

We live on a lovely location by the water and in winter when there are no leaves on the trees, we can see Windsor Castle from our house. We think this is God's own spot. We were thinking of downsizing, but the views are something else and we'd miss it too much. Ham Island has always been a great place to come home to. I'm very lucky. I think the luck factor has enormous influence on anything you do, whatever your job is. If you've had a bit of good luck – which I've had plenty of – it can make a hell of a difference. I think living on this island is part of my luck too.

Lion Island

A tiny, wooded and uninhabited island only accessible by boat, Lion Island is owned
by The Crown Estate, the organisation that runs the Queen's land.

Size and location:
Approximate size: 1,500m²
Coordinates: 51.4693, -0.5796

Can you visit?
No, the island is privately owned.

Carl's tips:
*You can spot Lion Island from the Thames Path on the Old Windsor riverbank, although
it's heavily wooded and often difficult to spot.*

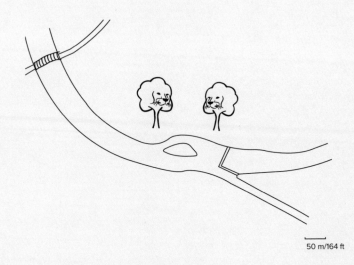

50 m/164 ft

Sumptermead Ait

A narrow, uninhabited island just beyond Victoria Bridge (King Edward VII Avenue) in Datchet, Sumptermead Ait is owned by The Crown Estate and leased to Datchet Golf Club behind it. A random selection of famous faces have been spotted playing golf at Datchet Golf Club, including Bing Crosby, the boxer Sugar-Ray Robinson and Prince Andrew. Much further back in history, the island was given to the St Helen's nunnery in 1263. Three centuries later, it was leased to the Queen's laundress in 1586.

Size and location:
Approximate size: 1,000m²
Coordinates: 51.489, -0.591

Can you visit?
No, the island is leased by Datchet Golf Club.

Carl's tips:
Have a look at the island from the Thames Path, which runs through The Home Park – a huge and beautiful Royal park – on the opposite bank.

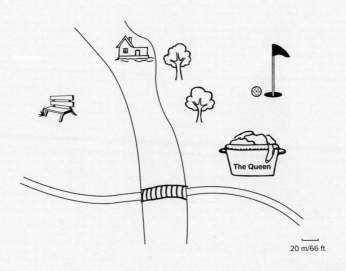

The Queen

20 m/66 ft

Black Potts Ait

Only accessible by boat, this overgrown and uninhabited island has part of the Black Potts Railway Bridge running overhead. In the past, it was a favourite area for fishing for Charles II, author and diplomat Sir Henry Wotton and Tudor writer John Hales. It was an area full of eels too and eel bucks (baskets) have been found in the area.

Size and location:
Approximate size: 4,750m²
Coordinates: 51.493, -0.597

Can you visit?
Yes, the island is accessible by boat in theory, although it's so overgrown it's difficult to walk on.

Carl's tips:
Look across the river from the Thames Path to catch a glimpse of this island.

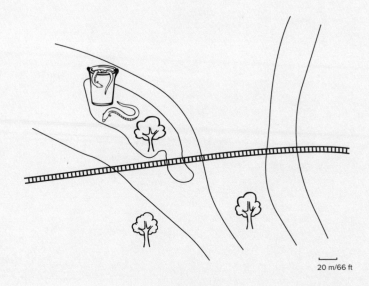

20 m/66 ft

Romney Eyot

This long thin island is totally uninhabited. Romney Eyot has a path surrounded by grass and a few trees. Nearby Eton College bought the eyot in the 1840s to prevent the building of the railway bridge planned over the island. The railway bridge went to Black Pott's Ait next door instead. An annual Eton boating regatta started at Romney Eyot in 1888 to commemorate a visit of King George III.

Size and location:

Approximate size: 26,000m²
Coordinates: 51.491, -0.605

Can you visit?

Yes, just walk across the lock onto the island.

Carl's tips:

Get the best view of the island from the Thames Path. On the opposite riverbank, spot the grounds of Eton College.

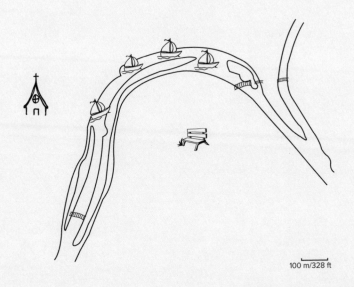

100 m/328 ft

Cutler's Ait

This island is attached to Romney Eyot by a weir and attached to the mainland by a couple of wooden foot bridges. The island was previously home to an ancient mill – Tangier Mill – famous for making clay smoking pipes. The island is now owned by Eton College and has a series of pathways that lead to intimate gardens with benches and pavilions.

Size and location:

Approximate size: 7,000m²
Coordinates: 51.490, -0.606

Can you visit?

Yes, just walk across one of the bridges onto the island.

Carl's tips:

Walk alongside Romney Eyot and Cutler's Ait on the Thames Path to arrive in central Windsor, right by Windsor Castle.

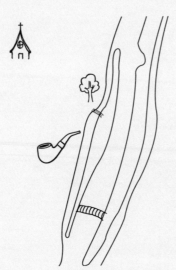

50 m/164 ft

Firework Ait

This tiny, tree-covered island just past Windsor Bridge got its name from the fireworks display held annually on it, which was part of the Eton regatta on 4 June. The festivities later moved up to Romney Eyot and Firework Ait became a little neglected. This is said to be the island where the poet Shelley used to row his skiff to from Eton.

Size and location:
Approximate size: 400m²
Coordinates: 51.4852, -0.6105

Can you visit?
Yes, accessible by boat.

Carl's tips:
Get a good view of the island from Windsor Bridge, or walk directly alongside it on the pretty promenade of the Thames Path. Browns Windsor (The Promenade, Barry Avenue, SL4 1QX) across the road has outdoor seating on two levels from which you can see the island too.

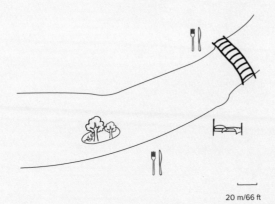

20 m/66 ft

Snap Ait

This small, wooded and uninhabited island is very close to the Thames towpath. It's home to greenery, some waterfowl and a fishing jetty.

Size and location:
Approximate size: 2,000m²
Coordinates: 51.485, -0.613

Can you visit?
Yes, accessible by boat.

Carl's tips:
Walk alongside this island from the Thames Path, then stop for a refreshment at the Cafe Barry kiosk on the riverbank and take a stroll across the road in the pretty Alexandra Park.

20 m/66 ft

Deadwater Ait

This is another uninhabited island with a railway bridge running overhead, and brick arches underneath. From the 1860s to the mid 20th century, it was a designated river swimming spot, complete with changing rooms next to the railway arches and handrails leading into the water. After swimming pools were developed on the mainland, the island became parkland. Accessed by a footbridge, it's still a park to this day. Look out for one of the best views of Windsor Castle in the local area.

Size and location:
Approximate size: 15,750m²
Coordinates: 51.486, -0.618

Can you visit?
Yes, just walk over the footbridge.

Carl's tips:
Circle the island on the water by hiring a kayak from the nearby Canoe and Kayak Tours (Barry Avenue, SL4 5JA; www.canoeandkayaktours.co.uk) or London Kayak Tours (Windsor Leisure Centre, Stovell Road, SL4 5JB; www.londonkayaktours.co.uk).

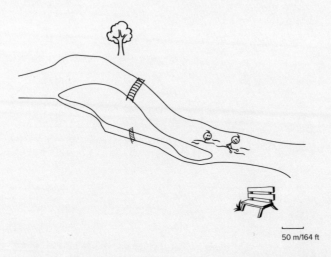

50 m/164 ft

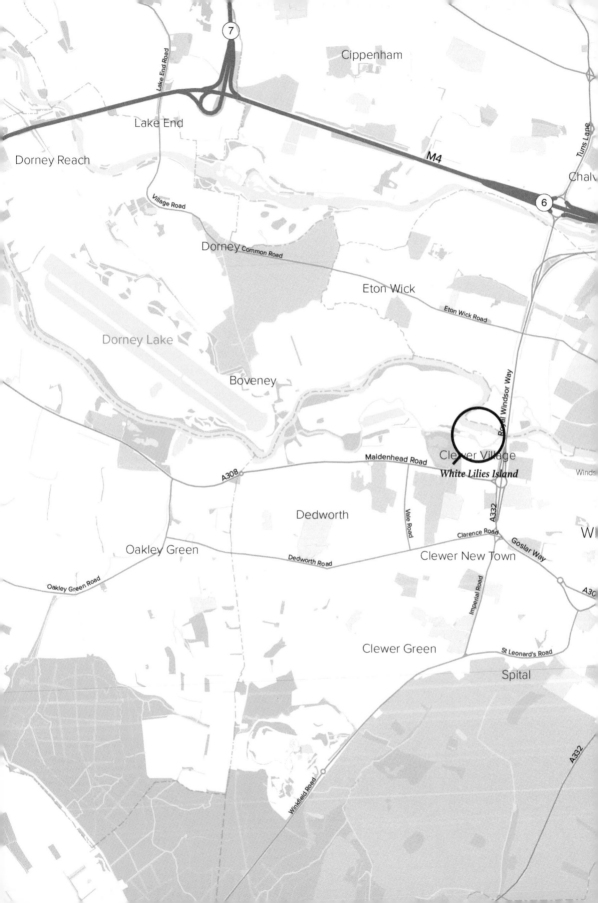

White Lilies Island

This is a peninsula rather than an island and is accessed by a road bridge. It has just a handful of large, exclusive houses on it. Former *Neighbours* actress and musician Natalie Imbruglia lived on the island and named her second album White Lilies Island after it.

Size and location:
Approximate size: 14,500m²
Coordinates: 51.487, -0.626

Can you visit?
Yes, just drive over the road bridge, although there isn't much to see as there are just a few large, private residences.

Carl's tips:
Have a look at the island from the Thames Path on the Eton side of the river.

50 m/164 ft

Boveney Lock Island

Boveney Lock Island

This island opened its current lock in the 1830s, although the original lock is thought to date back to the 1500s. Nowadays it just has a small lock keeper's cottage and gardens. The island is attached to Windsor Racecourse by a weir. The racecourse is also an island – but not a River Thames island – as it is cut off from the mainland by Clewer Mill Stream on the other side.

Size and location:
Approximate size: 5,000m²
Coordinates: 51.491, -0.641

Can you visit?
No, only those using the lock can access the island.

Carl's tips:
Walk along the Thames Path on the Eton side of the river to walk directly alongside the lock island for great views of the racecourse over the river.

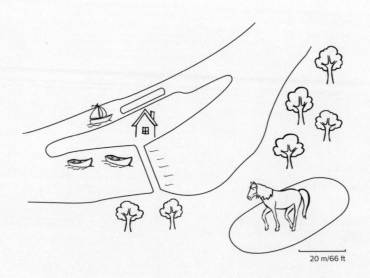

20 m/66 ft

Bush Ait

This small uninhabited, thickly wooded island sits at the tip of the Windsor Racecourse island.

Size and location:
Approximate size: 6,500m²
Coordinates: 51.487, -0.648

Can you visit?
Yes, accessible by boat.

Carl's tips:
The Thames Path on the Eton side of the river gives a great view of the island. A wide open nature reserve – Sutherland Grange – runs alongside the island on the other side of the river, although the thickly wooded riverbank makes it difficult to see.

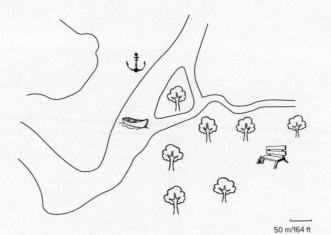

50 m/164 ft

Queen's Eyot

This island has been owned by Eton College since the 1920s. It's accessed by a private chain ferry and has a pristine clubhouse at the centre of the island, surrounded by gardens and dense woodland. College schoolboys use the island for recreational activities. It's also available for hire for private parties and weddings.

Size and location:
Approximate size: 23,000m²
Coordinates: 51.496, -0.680

Can you visit?
No, not unless you hire the clubhouse out!

Carl's tips:
Walk directly alongside Queen's Eyot on the Thames Path by Dorney Lake.

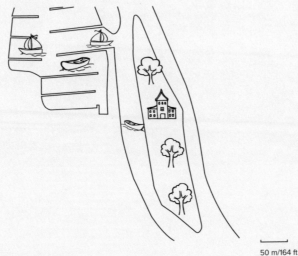

50 m/164 ft

Anthony Johnson
Island Facilities Manager

Former serviceman Anthony has been living and working on Queen's Eyot – a venue owned by Eton College – since 2014.

How did you discover Queen's Eyot?

I'm a former serviceman and spent 22 years in the Grenadier Guards. A former Grenadier Guardsman, Lieutenant Colonel Richard Dorney, realised it was difficult for previous servicemen to find jobs and set up a website where jobs could be advertised only to us. He phoned up firms to convince them to advertise any vacancies they had on this website. Many former officers for The Household Division – the army regiments serving the Queen – went to Eton College, so they really believed in Lieutenant Colonel Dorney's venture. I was looking on the website for a job one day and saw a role advertised to become the Facilities Manager of Queen's Eyot, which is owned by Eton College. I applied, got the job, and I've been living and working here since 2014.

What does your job involve?

Queen's Eyot is a venue that can be hired for events and weddings over the summer. During that time of year, my job is mostly about maintenance to keep the grounds and venue in perfect working order. A lot of my summers are spent mowing the grass. I use a pedestrian mower because it gives a better cut of grass compared to the ride-on mower, and I think people who hire the venue deserve the best. But it means I spend three hours a day, three times a week cutting grass! Since Queen's Eyot is a boat-only island, I also operate the ferry for the events, transporting staff, guests and everything that needs to be brought over to the island, from wedding cakes to decorations. I also provide security, patrolling the island every day of the year and help keep guests safe at events.

What are weddings on the island like?

They're exceptional. I have a strong connection with each couple straight away, because when they're interested in booking the island, I'm the one giving the tour. So when their big day comes around, I always dress up in an Eton blue waistcoat with a fleur-de-lys on it and a boater hat. One of my favourite spots on the island is a bench at the end, which has wonderful views. I always recommend the happy couple wanders down there to spend 15 minutes together, because otherwise the day goes so quickly. They always love it. I've taken many-a-photographer out on the boat to get a perfect photo of them from the water, with the island backdrop behind them.

What happens on the island when there isn't a wedding going on?

It's used a lot for corporate functions and quite a few of them do dragon boat racing as part of the day out. They go to the end of the island and race down – it's great to watch. During the winter, I mainly do the hard maintenance on the island. The college has put me on all sorts of courses so I can manage things like taking down trees if necessary. Throughout the year, the college uses it for other events too. House barbecues are popular, as it gives the staff and boys from each house a chance to get together. The boys play rugby and football on the huge lawn, then they'll all have something to eat. There's also a wonderful Eton College tradition where the boys can use the island for something called 'absence'. They'll row up to the island, which takes around an hour. Then they spend another hour on the island for 'chocolate, pop and crisps', as they call it. Then they row back for when the register is called. Years ago, when the boys rowed up here, they used to be given a pint of beer, because in those days the beer was purer than the water!

What did your wife say when you told her you wanted to live on an island?

She assumed there must be a bridge. People often confuse Queen's Eyot with the next island along – Monkey Island – which has a footbridge. That's where my wife thought we were going to live if I got the job. So it was a bit of a shock when we got here! She absolutely loves it though.

Has the island ever flooded?

Most winters, the pontoon disappears under water. It's never been very bad, but that's the reason we don't take bookings for weddings in the winter. It would be awful to have to phone a bride to tell her we've had to close the venue. We have a permanent mooring in Bray Marina in case the water ever gets too high, but that hasn't happened so far.

Have you discovered any interesting stories about the island?

Decades ago, about 30,000 tonnes of rubble was bought to the island to lift it, hence why it doesn't tend to flood. I also discovered the island itself was sold to Eton College by Colonel Victor Van de Weyer in 1923, for a price of 10 shillings! Unfortunately, the original clubhouse burned down in 1988. If you look around the clubhouse today, some of the aquatic rolls are pitted and blistered. This is from where the firemen managed to save some of the artefacts. Rather than throw them away, the college put them up for provenance.

What's the best thing about living on the island?

People can't just turn up at our front door – everyone has to make a phone call and ask us to collect them in the boat. It's worth its weight in gold when you have a mother-in-law! The island is our paradise and we've never been so alone before. I'm passionate about the place, hence why I mow the lawn so diligently over the summer! I absolutely love it and feel like I'm living the dream.

What's the worst thing about living on the island?

Running out of milk can be a hassle. Especially when you get to the car to drive to the shop, only to realise you've left the car keys behind, and you have to get the boat back over to the island get them. There are practical elements to living on an island that you don't have to think of when you live elsewhere. Every month or two I have to get a huge canister of gas over from the mainland to the island – these are very bulky and heavy. And if my wife goes out in the evening, I can't go to bed until she's home because I have to pick her up in the boat.

What do you do when you're not taking care of the island?

This is a great stretch of river to go fishing, which I'm really keen on, but I've only gone fishing a handful of times since I've lived here. There's always something else to do on the island. Watching the wildlife is fascinating too. There are two deer on the island, pheasants, herons and the occasional adder swimming across the water. I've fed the swans by hand too. They swim down from Windsor where there are lots of people, so they don't seem to be frightened of humans.

What's the most bizarre thing that has happened to you on the island?

My Labrador dog misjudged the gap between the pontoon and the boat one January, and fell in the river. I managed to get hold of him, but by the time I'd done that, the boat had drifted away. So I took off my two jackets, dived into the river and got the boat. It's lucky I was the Army champion for the 100-metre butterfly! There's a video of the whole thing on YouTube, called 'Man Saves Dog – Then Regrets It'. Although I didn't regret it at all!

Have you taken any other unexpected dips in the river?

My wife and I both fell in the river one winter. The date was Friday 13, believe it or not. My wife went to the back of the boat to unmoor it, slipped and fell in. I came running from the front of the boat, and slipped and fell in too! The river was flowing quite fast that day, so it was quite a job to get to the boat and get ourselves back aboard. My wife's run a few marathons and at the time she was training for the London Marathon. I told her all she needed to do after the river incident was cycling, then she'd have done her triathlon too. Apparently that wasn't funny... So between us and the dog, it's 4-0 to the river so far.

Find out more about Queen's Eyot at www.queenseyot.co.uk

Monkey Island

The name of this famous island evolved from Monk's Eyot, named after the monks who resided at a nearby abbey. The island enjoys a higher position than many other islands on the River Thames, as rubble from the Great Fire of London was dumped here in 1666. The third Duke of Marlborough bought the island in 1738. He built a fishing lodge (now known as the Pavilion) and a fishing temple. He also commissioned a French artist, Andien de Clermont, to paint odd pictures of monkeys on the lodge's ceiling. These monkeys are shown wearing clothes and doing human activities, including fishing, boating and shooting on the river.

Although the island has changed ownership since the Duke died in 1758, it has almost always been an inn or hotel ever since. In the 1800s, it became fashionable for wealthy people to visit islands such as these. Edward II and Queen Alexandra visited Monkey Island frequently for afternoon tea with their children – all of whom were to become reigning monarchs in the future. H.G. Wells also rowed to the island for secret meetings with his lover, the author Rebecca West. Her first novel – *Return of the Soldier* – also mentions the island. English composer, Sir Edward Elgar, frequently visited the island too.

The footbridge was installed in the 1950s and remains today. The island has changed ownership a number of times since, with improvements and renovations made along the way. The Birmingham Six – a group of men who wrongly received life sentences for pub bombings – spent their first night of freedom on the island in 1991.

The island – which has some Grade I listed buildings – is undergoing a major refurbishment. The new luxurious hotel is due to have a signature restaurant, a stylish bar and a lounge for afternoon tea. A spa will be located on a converted Dutch barge.

Size and location:
Approximate size: 22,500m²
Coordinates: 51.503, -0.683

Can you visit?
Yes, once the refurbishment is complete.

Carl's tips:
Walk alongside the island on the Thames Path on the Dorney side of the river. There's also a footbridge that crosses the river in between Queen's Eyot and Monkey Island, offering another viewing point of both islands.

Thames Path

The Thames Path is a long-distance footpath that follows the course of the River Thames in its entirety. While a towpath has existed on many stretches of the river for centuries, the Thames Path – running the whole length of the Thames – only officially opened in 1996. An amazing 184 miles long, from the source of the Thames in Gloucestershire to the Thames Barrier in south east London, walking the length of the Thames has become a popular challenge.

Many of the River Thames islands in this book are visible from the Thames Path. When it's not possible to visit an island directly, we encourage you to wander along the Thames Path and go island-spotting along the way. Together with our insights into the lives of modern-day island dwellers and incredible historical island tales from past times, there's no better way to witness a truly original way of living near the city.